Intr

He who overcomes

Conquerors will march in the victory parade, their names indelible in the Book of Life. I'll lead them up and present them by name to my Father and His Angels - Revelation 3:5 MSG

In June of 1980, I asked Jesus to come into my life. I had become intensely aware that something was missing. The Jesus I was taught about in Sunday School was no longer enough. The story of anyone allowing himself to die on a cross goes deeper than those adorable pictures. So I spent the beginning days of my "true" salvation devouring books written by *Kenneth Copeland, Kenneth E. Hagin, R. W. Shambach, Dave Roberson, Joyce Meyer, Jerry Savelle, Novel Hayes, Frederick K. C. Price* and *Jesse Duplantis*, to name a few. The deeper I searched, the more God filled my cup with His knowledge.

In 1982, God called me into His five-fold ministry as a teacher. I was bold enough to start a home bible study and green enough to only be able to teach the difference between salvation and just going to church. I taught just what I had learned; there's much more to that cross than you realize.

In January of 1983, I met a true servant of God at *God's Little Greenhouse* Bookstore, named Lola Daniels. She introduced me to *Word of Life Center* when I revealed to her that I was waiting on God to direct me to a church that taught the true word of God. Thirty-two years later, I remain under the tutorship of *Pastor Sam Carr* as I press on.

My growth in God's Word didn't turn all the grass in my life green, but it did instill in me a determination that I would never quit no matter the battle faced. At some points, I have asked God how long must I endure? When will I catch a break? A breath of fresh air? A moment to exhale? It became apparent that while life with my Savior was filled with great joy, I was still on the enemy's turf and there was a war declared to destroy my faith.

Warrior

God didn't use the actual word *warrior* when referring to me until 2009, but I knew I had been given the boldness and discernment to stand in the gap for others. My heart was for the hurting and standing against the wicked one became a pleasure. Having endured so many challenges in my own life had taught me one thing, it won't be easy, but God will never fail you.

In a world far beyond my physical sight lies many layers of complications that only my Heavenly Father sees. All the years we have wallowed in the muck of the world's ways has piled layers upon layers of pains, traditions, and corruptions in our souls. I took my issues and crossed paths with others and their issues and out of it, we made a mess.

However, I saw the chisel in God's hands ready to free me from life's bondages. I must acknowledge though, His work in my life could not have begun without my willingness to bow my soul at the foot of His cross. As I voluntarily allowed Him, He's chipped away, a layer at a time, until like a baby chick breaking through its shell, I came forth free from things that had kept me bound. My trips to the Cross were many and the count continues to grow even today as I realize the Chiseler's job is far from done. I have at times resisted God's hand as He chipped away at life's layers. It has not been easy since I did not always understand His ways. As years passed, I grew stronger in accepting my fate blindly as each trip to the cross taught me I could trust Him. A wounded child has emerged a warrior, knighted by God, to help other hurting people.

    This book may have been birthed in my soul in 1998, but it has taken years of living life to write it. Fifty plus years, in fact, has taught me that truly the things we suffer aren't easy, but in order to reach the mountaintops, they're necessary.

To Mom

The Experiences We Live

I could not begin to write this book without first saying, I have the absolute greatest mom in the world. I can truly say, you did the best you knew how.

I remember having this conversation with you and your first cousin as we drove home from Biloxi, Mississippi one summer afternoon. We had just finished having what turned out to be our last visit with an aunt, who went home to be with the Lord a short time later. You and your cousin were reminiscing about your moms, who were sisters. I could hear the pain in your tones but also the anger. Life and its twisted path had not been kind and the wounds were as obvious then as they were in the 1950s.

You were both furious as you exchanged stories of the details buried deep within your souls. Rightfully so, no child deserved to have to live receiving the aftermaths of someone else's misfortunes. Regrettably though, it happens. Every day of someone's life, they pay the price of another's pain. Hurting people really do hurt people, especially, the ones they love.

In the midst of the conversation, compassion for your moms came over me and I said, "they did the best they knew how." Life for them ain't been no crystal stairs either. (Derived from Langston Hughes' poem, Mother to Son). Being born on a sharecroppers' property put them in a state of freedom without really being free. It was hard for our ancestors to live their lives only one step out of slavery. The scars on their backs were not the only reminders for some of them. For my mother's mother, being mulatto filled her life with hatred from both white and black races. She was a reminder to the Caucasian race that the boss crossed over, and to the African American race that the boss crossed over and there was nothing they could do about it. Life for her ain't been no crystal stairs. She did the best she knew. All that anger spilled over onto you, even though you were her rock. Hurting people hurt the ones that love them.

Little did I know, one day the Lord would remind me that you too did the best you knew how. We were so different in personalities. You were a fixer, but I didn't need fixing. I was a touchy feely person, but you didn't need touches. You were a great provider. You worked your fingers to the bone for us, but...you didn't hear me cry behind closed doors when I didn't know how to tell you I didn't need "fix it mom," I just needed mom.

I can't write this book without exposing my pains which includes your pains. Please realize that I respect you and your struggles more than you know.

Life doesn't come wrapped in a package that we would have designed, it doesn't even come as God originally designed. It just comes with all it joys and miseries. Thank you for never deserting this journey! Thank you for being the best mom you knew to be.

IT AIN'T EASY BUT IT'S NECESSARY

by Mary J Pickens

Contents

Introduction..1

To Mom...5

Prologue..11

Chapter One - Abandoned by My First Love...........13

Chapter Two - Sins Uncovered.........................27

Chapter Three - Transitioning Alone..................37

Chapter Four - High School Sweetheart................45

Chapter Five - A Time to Heal........................57

Chapter Six - At the Feet of Jesus...................63

Chapter Seven - God, I Quit..........................75

Chapter Eight - I AM LOVE............................83

Chapter Nine - Love is Kind..........................95

Chapter Ten - Old Wounds............................111

Chapter Eleven - Through the Valley of Death.......119

Chapter Twelve - Too Soon...........................147

Chapter Thirteen - I'll Never Forget................153

Acknowledgements....................................159

Reference...163

Notes...165

It Ain't Easy...But It's Necessary

Prologue

I was flabbergasted when we, the workers of <u>The Soldiers of Compassion Ministry</u> Outreach Team, gathered for a meeting of protocol with Tina Rivera, co-founder of the ministry. She announced that I was the one God placed on her heart to speak at the upcoming Thanksgiving outreach dinner.

Surprisingly, when I asked the Holy Spirit what topic was I going to minister about, He said as clear as a church bell ringing at noon, "It Ain't Easy...But It's Necessary." The title was so striking that chills ran down my spine. I remember a whisper that echoed within me, "This is only the beginning."

After speaking at the outreach dinner where I delivered the sermon of the title just as the Holy Spirit instructed, God told me this would be the title of a book I would one day write. Book? Write? Me?

At the next Sunday's church service that followed the banquet, Yolanda Gilyard, a fellow member of the outreach team, expressed how much she was blessed by the words I spoke, then she proceeded to blurt out that, "You're going to write a book on that same subject, *It Ain't*

Easy...But It's Necessary. I feel it, I just know," she went on to say. Just like Mary, the mother of Jesus, I quietly pondered in my heart the words she spoke over and over again. Who me? Disbelief flooded my mind as I marveled how someone like me would dare to dream of writing a pamphlet, let alone a book. Despite the disbelief, I had to acknowledge, she had just unknowingly confirmed the words I heard earlier in the center of my being.

IT AIN'T EASY, BUT IT'S NECESSARY
Chapter One
Abandoned by My First Love

March of 1957, almost fifty-seven years to the date this story began, as a spirit of darkness came in and flipped my world upside down. Some of this story will be told from the memories of others as it was told to me. I was only three months old when this event occurred.

How it all started

Situated in the red clay hills and the deep pine tree forest, appearing on the map as only a tiny dot, was the town of Grambling. Located in Lincoln parish, 23 acres soon gave way to the establishment that all would come to know as Grambling College. Established as an industrial and agricultural school in 1901, its reputation rapidly grew as a strong football legend, for its world renowned band, and a melting pot for teachers. So goes the story of how my parents met.

A strong, well-built, muscular, football star, heavily recruited from Shreveport, Louisiana, laid eyes on a ninety-eight pound beauty who grew up just eighteen miles east of him in Haughton, Louisiana. As they walked across the college campus of the now world famous Grambling State University, he began to eyeball this "fresh meat" that was just beginning the adult phase of her life. Needing a way to introduce himself to her, he used the ploy that no freshmen were allowed to walk across the courtyard in front of the athletic building, but had to walk around. Arthur informed her that her penalty would be that he would have to dunk her head in the fountain. Dorothy quickly replied, "Go ahead, my hair needs shampooing anyway."

Over a span of time at college, my parents began to run in the same circle of friends, where my dad would often tease my mother by acting out in front of his fellow teammates. They found themselves attending the same outings between Grambling and Shreveport and Bossier City. Eventually their friendship budded into a romance that led to a marriage and the birth of my brother and me.

My brother, Arthur, Jr. was born on March 30, 1955, at 7:45 in the a.m., weighing seven pounds, four ounces. I was born at 7:45 p.m. and weighed seven pounds four ounces. I was always fascinated that my brother and I were both born at exactly 7:45, me in the p.m. and Arthur in the a.m. and we both weighed exactly the same. Other than time and birth weight, my brother and I had no other physical characteristics that would lead one to believe we were even related. Arthur, Jr. was the spitting image of my dad with a few features of my mom. I, on the other hand, had no real resemblance to either of my parents, nor anyone else in our immediate family, as a matter of fact.

Trust

My dad was drafted into the United States Army and was deployed to serve a tour of duty in the Korean War. During his absence, I was born and was around three months old when he arrived back in the States safely.

Life was no different for us than any other military family. The spouse left behind had to hold down the fort. That generally consisted of maintaining the house, working, raising the kids, and worrying about their mate returning home on their feet instead of in a body bag. The soldier, on the other hand, worried if his wife would wait patiently and faithfully for his return. Trust was a valuable commodity for a soldier's family. Upon dad's return, the devil planted a seed of discord in our home through his friend's harmless joking. Proverbs 16:18 states that, *"Pride goes before destruction."* My dad's pride blinded him temporarily. He laughed at the time, but later it became obvious that he allowed the thoughts to ferment in his mind.

The Milkman's Baby

After settling back into home life, a conversation about the money my mom had saved from her military allotment came into play. Her purpose of saving was for my dad to return to Grambling to complete his senior year. You see, Dad's status of being a college student presented no barrier to Uncle Sam's claim that the army needs you. However, dad didn't want to return to school and felt the money would be best spent on a car. Mom, however, stood her grounds as she felt there were other needs the money could be used for more important than purchasing a car. Deceitfully, dad had a relative forge my mom's name to buy a vehicle anyway. As he gloated about his successful transaction, the disagreement became heated. As dad began to leave, in his anger, he turned and looked at me as

I sat in the high chair, and said, "As far as I know, she could be "The Milkman's Baby."

Earlier, while drinking and horse playing around, my dad's buddies were the first to say I was too cute to be his and I must be the "The Milkman's Baby." My mother laughed when she heard their remark. She knew them well enough to know they were not serious. Without regard to the consequences though, in anger, my dad let those words come out of his mouth. Instantly, regret was already apparent as he had to bolt for a way to escape the lunging butcher's knife my mother was swinging toward him since the chicken she was cutting up had lost center stage and he was now her target. According to mom, upon hearing his words, she immediately felt as if she was having an out of body experience. She chased him throughout the house as she swung the knife at him in such a rage, that twice, she was able to slice his shirt tail, front and back. My brother, grabbing her leg, slowed her just enough to give my dad an opportunity to sprint for the front door as she buried the knife in it. After retrieving the knife, my mother continued the chase outside where my grandmother's arrival home became my dad's saving grace. She pushed my dad behind her as she embraced my hysterical, knife flaring mother all the while dragging her back into the house. Through much struggle and persistence, she managed to bring her back to reality to the screams of her children. "He's not worth you going to jail, he's not worth it," my grandmother insisted.

That phrase, "The Milkman's Baby," caused more damage in two women's lives than the world would ever know.

A Slap in the Face

Feeling betrayed by her first love, my dad's remarks put my mom's character and honor on trial. I'm sure she felt people were constantly looking at me to determine whose side they would take. Today no one would blink an eye if a woman has two babies by different daddies, but in the 1950's that was considered a disgraceful secret which was usually hidden and taken to ones' grave. The pain and embarrassment drove a wedge not only between my parents, but also between me and the one who should have been my first love, my mom, and the one who should have been my protector, my dad.

Years Passed

One spring in Shreveport, it seemed like it rained for 40 days. The flooding became so severe that we made national news. Dad called Arthur, Jr. to see if he was being affected by the flood. I lived in the same city as my brother did, but dad never called to check on me nor made any inquiries about my safety. Unconsciously, each time my brother made a remark about his interactions with dad, he broke my heart. I don't think he ever knew that dad had never in my life called me.

After years of dealing with my dad's egocentric attitudes, in desperation, I asked my mother was he truly my dad. It was not my intention to disrespect her, I was just searching for the reasons why my father didn't love me. He made such a distinct difference between my brother and me. Secretly, in my heart, I wanted my mom to say he wasn't my dad. At least then I would be able to understand his inability to connect with me on an honest level. This request did not sit well with my mom. I offended her and she told me in some very colorful words that she knew who had fathered her children. She was proud to say that she had only known one man in her lifetime and the possibility of a milkman, or anyone else other than Arthur was zero. My dad's reckless speech had crossed that invisible line that cost us everything, and in my searching for clarity, I crossed it too.

Branded

My mother has never been an emotional person. She didn't show a lot of happiness or pain. Her greatest expression was anger. That emotion, she displayed repeatedly and that's the only way she ever expressed her feelings toward my being called the "Milkman's Baby." "No man is going to call my baby ..." was all she said.

I was branded the "Milkman's Baby." Every story I was ever told involving my dad and me always at some point ended with the mentioning of that tale. No one ever included the analogy of the adult version of the truth, that my dad's words questioned my mom's faithfulness. I always thought that the milk was in reference to my skin tone (my dad has a darker complexion), not in reference to another man doing more then delivering milk on his rounds.

Amazingly, the same buddies that started that confusion, came to my mother after hearing about my parent's breakup, and apologized. They all said, out of all the women in their circle, she was the one that no one would ever suspect of doing anything like that. They were offended that my dad had taken their ribbing that far, and told him so.

To his credit, my dad made many attempts to rectify his wrongs against my mom but his words always fell on deaf ears. Mom often told me that the pressure she felt from her mom prevented her from even entertaining the idea of reconciling her marriage. My grandmother telling her, "You don't let a man insult your child," stood in the way of my mom ever forgiving my dad. Once again, the break up pointed to me, and now I am assuming that there were a lot of words left out of those conversations when I was around because it was grown folks business. The final story, as told to me, always ended with my mom defending my honor with the heroic measure of the butcher knife victory. However, the knife that never touched my dad's body, scarred my heart for over a half a century, as the scarlet brand seemed to deem me as an outcast in my family's heart, and most importantly, in my mother's broken heart.

Abandoned

My mom's lack of connection with me was always blamed on my independence. I held my bottle early, walked early, and in doing so, I was the total opposite of my brother who was sickly and needy. She felt I didn't need her, but I did need her. For years I longed to be a part of my family; which included my mother, my grandmother, my brother, but I stood on the outside looking in. Trying to secure a place in their hearts proved to be so tiresome. I wanted my mom's eyes to light up when she saw me like they lit up when she saw my brother. I needed her to applaud my life's accomplishments. Please, let my life stand for more than just existing. I didn't make the mistake but it cost me dearly.

Finally, as a teenager, I stopped trying to fit in and accepted the truth that I was just a dependent, according to the IRS, who was being cared for by everything money could or should buy but... never really loved. They loved me, but they were never in love with me. I mattered, but I didn't. The intimacy I craved from my mother was nonexistent. We were in the same world but never together. I retreated to my bedroom, a place of seclusion where I was somebody. The words on the recordings of Aretha Franklin, Gladys Knight & the Pips, and the likes, were a comfort to me. I rode that midnight train to Georgia over and over as I learned to escape my feelings and not care about life on the other side of my door as it went on without me.

It was a strange pattern that went on in my family. The boy children were preferred over the girls. My uncle was preferred over my mother, but she obviously accepted it as the way things should be, because she did nothing to break the curse. The girls in my family were used as work horses while the boys sat on pedestals. The devil's scheme to eliminate the male as head of our family was working. My father was gone and my mother was grooming my brother to become a dependent man to be served. Little did she know that shielding him from life's hard knocks would cause him to abandon his duty as the protector of his own children one day.

Hind Sight

I have tried to reason that my mother was so consumed with pain and unbelief of what had transpired that the last thing she could do was love "me." She was angry and bitter for being forced into a life she hadn't signed up for. Choices, bigger than she could handle, had prevented her from keeping her vows of going through better or worse but she was not prepared to go through life alone as a divorced mother of two either. Mom never talked about her true feelings, but as a woman, I now can see clearly how devastating it was for her as she walked the streets of her neighborhood carrying a child on her hip whose facial features gave no proof to her claim that my father was my father.

For we do not wrestle against flesh and blood, but against principalities, against powers, against the rulers of the darkness of this age, against spiritual hosts of wickedness in the heavenly places. Ephesians 6:12

Looking back, with no knowledge that this scripture even existed, I can definitely testify that I was not wrestling with flesh. There was a division of darkness that stood wedged between me and my mother and me and my dad. Neither of them could grasp the desperation of my heart crying, "I am here and I'm not invisible. I need to feel like I belonged to somebody. Please, look past this partition at this woman with the childlike heart, waving a white flag. I only want one of you to look up long enough to see that while you lost a great deal during that foolish exchange which satan used to destroy your marriage, it cost me more!" I lost both my parents, my father totally, my mother emotionally and neither one of them could hear my cries. The devil stole my protectors. Living life alone was not easy.

It Ain't Easy, but It's Necessary
Chapter Two
Sins Uncovered

Apology

My father went about being who he was. It was his world and we were all just allowed to live in it. He lost the fight of winning my mother back, and never got into the fight to even care about me. Sadly, once again, we do not war against flesh and blood. My dad never loved me as his child, proving it in a number of ways, but mostly by never in the thirty-six years that he lived after my birth, of ever calling me or purposely spending time with me. Uncommon for him, when I was thirty years old, my dad, while visiting his mom in Shreveport, apologized for calling me the "Milkman's Baby." He told me that he didn't believe what he said and was wrong for saying it. He explained that he was angry at my mother and used me to get back at her. Honestly, I'm sure my dad did not voluntarily apologize on his own. I believe that he surrendered to the persuasion of my dear sweet grandmother. She, and the rest of my dad's family, always treated me with love. However, my time spent with them was minimal. They didn't reach out often because of my mom's mother's vigilant watch to keep my parents apart which kept everyone at bay.

I smiled in my dad's face and accepted his apology, but his meaningless words were a mockery. They were an assignment, a task for the soothing of his consciousness, an accomplishment he could take back to his mother so she could get off his case. After that apology, nothing changed. My brother and the other half-siblings fathered by my dad all had stories of him putting forth an effort to spend time with them. Just this past year in June of 2014, at a reunion with siblings, Quentin and Pela, it was heart wrenching to hear their stories and to know that I, his second oldest, didn't have one story of how ever he embraced me as his own.

Redeemed but Crashing

God allows the tears to come sometimes so the destruction that satan brings into our lives can come to the top and be healed

I was twenty-four years old when I had a true encounter with God. When the "apology" came, I already had six years of learning to walk in the light of God under my belt. Why then, was I straining with the thoughts of hating my dad on one hand, but desperately needing him on the other? My growth in God had armed me with the knowledge that it was demonic forces, satan, that had set out to destroy my family. However, that knowledge didn't eradicate the anger I felt. The hand that was dealt to me was not truly mine to play. I was forced into this game by ignorant grown people. A game that wasn't suitable for kids. I was angry at myself for loving my dad. Voiceless, I shouted at him in my head, *"YOU DIDN'T PROTECT ME! You, in your drunken state, always nursing your wants, your needs, left me naked and exposed. Your love of money brought evil into our home. You destroyed my mother's heart to the point that she couldn't love her own baby, not tenderly. I was an obligation, a responsibility. No one ever looked for me when I shut up in my room. There were no applauses for me. I became invisible at six months old when you branded me the 'Milkman's Baby.' I hate..."*

God never nursed my hurts to the point of letting me sulk for long. He knew that the same evil spirits that brought chaos into my life were also waiting for me to cave in and open another door to depression or deep-rooted hatred. I had carried that "Milkman's" tale in my heart long enough. It was a wound as open and raw now as it was years ago. God was bringing everything to a head once and for all in order to slay that old dragon.

Anyone who claims to live in God's light and hates a brother or sister is still in the dark. It's the person who loves brother and sister who dwells in God's light and doesn't block the light from others. But whoever hates is still in the dark, stumbles around in the dark, doesn't know which end is up, blinded by the darkness.
I John 2:11 (MSG)

Defined

Knowledge is powerful. One of the first things God had me lay at the foot of the cross was the title of "Milkman's Baby."

Therefore, if anyone is in Christ, he is a new creation; old things have passed away; behold, all things have become new.
II Corinthians 5:17

At the cross, God whispered to my soul, "Mary, hurts done to you by other people, whether intentional or unintentional, DO NOT DEFINE WHO YOU ARE NOW! I am your Father, you are a daughter of the living King. I do not see you as a milkman's baby. When you accepted My Son's sacrifice you were covered in His Blood, and now I AM your protector. Lay that branded name at the cross, and leave it there."

I would like to tell you that when I left that cross I left all those hurts there and never visited them again, but I didn't. Something would trigger me and I would enter the battlefield of my mind and war with those hurts, stimulating them to live again. After coming to my senses, in embarrassment, I would repent and take them back to the foot of the cross, walking away again. I would practice this pattern again and again. With much patience, My God never condemned me. He only encouraged me and taught me from my failures.

I didn't recognize that my desire to hear my dad's voice was a sign of healing, a sign that I had begun to forgive him. I was ashamed that I longed for my dad's attention. Why was I reaching into the shambles of my yesterdays? In my heart, I knew he was my dad and I assumed if he and I could form a loving relationship, then maybe everyone else would follow suit. I just wanted to feel like I belonged somewhere. Relinquishing my desire, I used the excuse that he never reached out to me to resist the urge to call him.

Knowing it was time for me to wade a little deeper, the Holy Spirit began His final push. He said, "Mary, call your dad, but never expect him to call you back." Strange order, isn't it! "But God,"I began to protest! Interrupting, God said, "Mary, you have grown enough that you know that I so loved this world that I gave My Son even though they didn't love Him, but still I gave Him because of My love, not theirs. It's okay to love your father despite his efforts. I do." With one swift movement of the sword, God cut off the head of that harassing and tormenting lizard. That statement set me free from the bondage of the give and take act. I was beating myself up for loving my dad. The lies he told me bothered me, but yet I loved him. He deserted me, he denied me; but years later, I still proudly called him dad. The world would have called me foolish, my own grandmother would have just called me a fool.

..."*God has made the wisdom of this world look foolish*" I Corinthians 1:20b (NLT)

I learned to give in spite of what was given to me and to be unashamed. Isn't that what Jesus did? Aren't we supposed to be Christ like? When God gave His only Son as a sacrifice for us, did He do it based on how we would receive His gift? No! God gave us His gift based on His love for us, despite how or if we would receive it. An all knowing God, knew many would reject His Gift, yet He gave for ALL! Why didn't Jesus only take the names of the ones who would receive Him to the cross? Why didn't He reject those who He knew would reject Him? It's simple! It was His gift to give to whosoever He willed, and Jesus chose ALL because God loved ALL. Adam's mistaken choice opened a door of evil to ALL; God's gift of Jesus, rectified Adam's wrong and connected mankind to God once again. Man was given a way to live a God filled-life, Jesus. If they chose not to accept His way, His gift, then at least they had a choice. I began to use this method to measure myself: what would Jesus do? He loved the unloveable. Jesus loved me, and I loved my dad...just because.

I began to call my dad whenever my heart longed to hear his voice. Surprisingly, our talks were soothing to my soul, and never burdensome afterward because I did just as the Spirit of God instructed. Even though my dad promised at the end of each conversation to call me back, I never expected him to, and until the day he died, he never did.

Saying Goodbye

Strangely, one day an old classmate of my dad's who happened to work at the same facility as I worked, stop by my station. He asked me how my dad was doing and when I replied half-heartedly, "Okay, I guess," he began to scold me for not looking after my dad. Confused, I questioned his concern for my business. He informed me that my father had cancer. When he saw the shocked look on my face, he realized I didn't know. Toward the end of our conversation, I thanked him for telling me, and he left understanding that my dad's stories of me were all fabricated and I had no real relationship with him at all.

I did call only to find out that Dad was actually sick. Here I was trying to bring comfort to a man who never spent one moment of his life doing anything for me. Through a course of calls I learned that my father had put his affairs in order and had made peace with God. Shortly afterward, I received a call informing me that he had checked himself out of the hospital AMA, and went home to die.

I traveled to Los Angeles to attend his funeral. I don't really know why, except that even though he never loved me, I loved him, and I wanted to pay my last respects. The closure was for me.

"Daddy, (Father, God), what's my natural daddy doing?" I would ask. *"Learning how to be a daddy to you once you get to heaven,"* He replied.

In counseling with other people who are victims of parental absences, victims of the empty promises to come by or to call, I share that statement, and each time I am amazed at the comfort it brings. Just like for me, satisfaction comes to them with the new found hope that one day their daddy may look at them as his baby girl or baby boy.

It Ain't Easy But It's Necessary
Chapter Three
Transitioning Alone

Covering

There were so many incidents in the past that pierced my heart. I am certain my life would have had a different outcome if somebody had only stepped up to parent me.

God's system sets coverings in motion in our lives. He knows of our existence even before the mother has her first symptom that there's a change taking place in her body. Upon confirmation that there's a new life forming within her belly, the mother takes over as the fetus' covering by taking vitamins, changing eating and sleeping patterns, making routine doctor visits, all in the name of bringing forth a healthy baby. After birth, it becomes the parents' responsibility to not only provide a safe and secure physical environment, but to also steer the child's spiritual, emotional, and mental development in the proper direction. Any area left unprotected by the designated overseer leaves a child vulnerable to the

Deceiver who works tirelessly to pull us away from God's Light.

When Adam sinned, sin entered the entire human race. Adam's sin brought death, so death spread to everyone, for everyone sinned. Romans 5:12 NLT

As a young girl, visiting the *country* was one of my greatest past times. At the tender age of nine, while visiting the *country*, I was approached by my great uncle. He was one of my favorite uncles because he was a risk taker. He would allow me to shave him with a straight razor. All the adults would come by and remark how foolish he was because I could accidentally cut his throat, but he would just shoo them away as I continued to practice my barbering skills.

One day, he approached me differently. He instructed me to go into the outhouse and wait for him, promising he would be there later. I trusted my uncle, but as a baffled nine year old, I found no appeal to going into a stinky old outhouse. In his efforts to further convince me, he made the statement that "it wouldn't hurt." "What wouldn't hurt?" I asked. Confused and still innocent to the facts of sex, his assurance of a painless trip to the outhouse brought no agreement to his proposal. The rest of the day was filled with child-like play as I participated in romping around my great grand parent's land with the other children.

Thinking nothing of my uncle's offer, I never found it necessary to reveal the contents of our conversation until there was a heated exchange between two adult women on another of those occasional visits. One defended my great uncle, declaring he would never proposition a child, while the other contended the child's claim would profit her nothing to lie. The exposure of my uncle's fetish came when he made his outhouse proposal to a teenager. So many innocent children have become victims of men and women preying on them for their sick gratifications. Thank God I escaped this senseless offer of rape because of the repulsiveness found in a smelly old outhouse.

Transitioning Alone

In the sixties, there were no magnet programs, so I was allowed to skip from the 5th grade to the 7th grade. My mom could not have known what a whirlwind this would throw my life into. I walked up to the seventh graders and they were talking about who had the biggest legs and who had a boyfriend. "What?" I inquired. I wanted to know where the playground was and did they have the skills to go down the sliding board standing up and what time did we play softball. With puzzled looks on their faces, they informed me that they didn't sweat. Flabbergasted, I remember standing by as they critiqued my leg size and placed me in order ranging from largest to smallest. Out-numbered, I soon gave up on my child-like fantasies of ever surfing on a sliding board again.

Boyfriend

My physical appearance outgrew my age and mental maturity by a great deal. People always assumed I was three to four years older than I actually was. One day a boy that had begun to notice me showed up at my house. "Mary, you have company." Much to my dismay, there standing in my living room, was the boy. What did he want, I thought? "Your mom said I could come visit you." With a baffled look on my face, I secretly found my mother to ask why she did that. "I thought you wanted him to come," she replied. "Mom, I don't like boys," I rebutted. "Oh!" she responded.

That was the most excruciating two hours of my life. I was a 12 year old eighth grader, sitting in the presence of a 15 year old sophomore scared out of my mind. Once again, I found myself being pushed into a phase of life that I was not even remotely prepared for. Here I was with a *boyfriend*. Whenever I saw him I was pleading with God for him not to come and talk to me. I was panic stricken as I tried desperately to straighten my pigeon toed feet because the girls told me that was not attractive. I was under so much pressure trying not to trip and fall down with my painfully straightened feet as I tried to get up the nerve to talk to him in public, all while secretly begging my Momma to *"please rescue me."*

By the time I became a freshman in high school, my high school boyfriend, now a junior, was complaining to my cousin that I wouldn't kiss him. My cousin came to me to report the complaint. I informed him that I didn't know how to kiss. I was far too afraid to ask the girls for fear they would laugh inexperienced me to shame. Appallingly, my cousin taught me how to kiss. After many blundered attempts, I finally succeeded in my experience of bells ringing and fireworks exploding as my *boyfriend* and I shared our first kiss. As childhood gave way to puberty, the beast of a woman had awakened, but I was still a child.

On my own, wading through this maze, confused but excited, I found a man for the first time in my life, who loved me. The revelation that had eluded me all my existence was now being fulfilled by a teenager. I now know that the fact that we lived in different cities was my salvation. There was never any sexual pressure from him. We only saw each other at games and on the rare occasion when he came over. Ma Bell kept us in constant contact and the distance kept a glassy-eyed young lady and a budding young man from ever crossing that line. It's hard to measure yesterday when you were that young, but regrettably, I ended up hurting him for no apparent reason. No one had ever shown me how to respect love or told me that it could last forever. I was given no manual, no guide: I was simply flying by the seat of my pants. One wrong turn had caused me to break my own glass slipper.

Spiraling out of Control

Unguided, I spent the rest of my high school years looking for love in all the wrong places. I traded in my Prince Charming for Slick Willy. He had more tricks up his sleeve than Houdini. Slick Willy also lived in another city that was close by, so word would travel that my Mr. Right was doing me wrong. We had our arguments about the rumors, but he always smoothed things over by presenting me center stage while the other girls were left waiting in the wings. What kind of life was that for a fifteen year old to be dealing with? I was singing the blues and telling him to be a "do right man" if he wanted to keep me, while graduation had freed him to pursue life as he pleased. It was peculiar, but I didn't go through the emotions of crying my eyes out. Having no passionate attachment to my parents had schooled me for the *"win some, lose some"* cycle. So at the ripe old age of fifteen, I moved on.

As twisted as my life began, emotionally, I began to settle more after having a boyfriend. The void of not feeling loved by my parents was being fulfilled by the teenage scenarios of love. It didn't, however, eliminate the lopsided life I lived within my household, it just made it more bearable. I was still the *other* child, but that became their sick business while I sat on the sidelines in amazement watching as my brother controlled the lives of my mother and grandmother.

Thankfully, all my relationships had longevity and distance. The duration kept me company and the distance kept me out of a lot of trouble for which I was destined, had we lived closer. I managed to skid through life into my senior year with minimal bruises and scars. However, the tide was about to change as the end of my senior year approached. For the first time, I had a boyfriend that not only lived in the same city as I did, but also attended the same school.

    Listening in as the girls talked about certain incidents that had happened to them, broadened my awareness of sex. Also, by agreeing to do some housekeeping, I was accidentally introduced to a world of erotic literature. The beast that I thought was awakened from my first kiss was nothing in comparison to this new found discovery. The books portrayed sexual acts as an expression of love. I wasn't naive to the acts of sex, but the illustrations that penetrated my mind, were now speaking to my body. None of the music artists who had become my caregivers in the privacy of my bedroom, ever explained to me how to deal with this new chapter of my life. I needed my mother to invade the world on the other side of my bedroom door. I needed her to be pulled into my atmosphere. I needed her help. I couldn't ask though, I was embarrassed and we didn't have that type of connection, we didn't have that trust.

It Ain't Easy, But It's Necessary
Chapter Four
High School Sweetheart

At the end of my junior year while attending Booker T. Washington High School, I decided to spend the first half of my day at school and the second half at the Caddo Career Center. Toward the end of that school year, during a down pour, I met the boy who would eventually become my husband, as he closed the door to the bus in my face. I have often heard that you usually dislike *the one* before you like them: Well this myth proved to be true.

Fast Forward 1973

Toward the end of my senior year a lot was happening. I did the typical things like ordering memory books, or invitations, applying to colleges, but also in my case, picking baby names. Unable to ever have *the talk* with my mother and just making decisions on my own, proved to be a wrong turn for my life. At sixteen, I graduated high school in May of 1973 and gave birth to my first daughter in July. Talk about a life changer, this was a catastrophe!

Getting pregnant before marriage was my only mistake, not my daughter's existence. She's been a treasure in my life, a very good gift from a shaky beginning. Well meaning friends gave my mother information about legal abortions that would have eradicated a mistake. Her existence was God's plan, my having sex before marriage was a miscalculation of her arrival. At sixteen, I was not legally an adult yet. I could not vote on amendments that affected her life. I could not pay for her immunizations, her formula, her food, her childcare. At sixteen, no matter what deeds I committed, I was still considered a child; one who gave birth to a child.

I had been accepted by four colleges and my dream was to attend college where I would major in Accounting. I loved math and ledgers and after having taken a Bookkeeping course in high school, my fate was sealed. I wanted to become a CPA. However, now there were two young girls' lives to consider. Mine and my infant daughter.

My mother generously offered to allow me to attend the University of my choice, while she kept the baby at home with her. As hospitable as this offer was, it was met with great resistance. I would not put my baby in the same shoes I wore. I would not allow her to look back at her life and feel that I deserted her. My heart was crushed at not attending school, but there are consequences to the decisions you make in life. I couldn't take the easy way out at the expense of my innocent child. So, I decided to attend school at a local college. Everything went well, except with an infant, you don't just throw on your backpack and head to class like most Freshmen. First, you prepare the bottles, make sure the diaper bag is stocked, dress the baby, then off you go to the sitter. After all of that, I was headed to class. Even though I was still the age of a child, my plate was full as I struggled to juggle the life of an adult.

My daughter's father and I, despite the pressures, had managed to stay together throughout our last year in high school and throughout the pregnancy and delivery. So when she was six months old we decided to get married.

On a wet and cold January evening, one month after I turned 17 and he turned 18, the parents of a healthy baby girl, exchanged matrimonial vows. My husband secured a job with his father, enabling the three of us to move into a cozy apartment known as the legendary *shotgun house*. It had a living room, one bedroom, a bath, and kitchen large enough for a dinette set. His parents gave us the furnishings for the living and dining rooms and my mother allowed me to bring my bedroom set, minus that girly canopy, and the baby's furniture to the start of our humble beginnings.

My husband had a strong foundation of taking on the responsibility of providing for his family and I quickly became well-schooled in making ends meet. So together, we set out to construct a life of forever.

Ten years later

Hindsight has taught me that a 17 and 18 year old should not get married. There's too much of the unknown to unveil and that short life span does not allow for such discoveries. Our marriage in the eyes of some was good. We had our struggles during our small beginnings, but we were also making great strides. By the ages of 20 and 21, we owned two houses and had added two boys to our family. I was a baby making machine that no birth control could stop. Four years later, we were earning close to $60,000 a year. That was extremely good for the early eighties. We traveled and exposed our children to life outside of our neighborhood and culture. Then suddenly, it all came to a screeching halt.

February 1984

After ten years of marriage, I asked my husband for the last time to leave our home or I would. He had resisted our separating for the last three years, but I would no longer allow him to delay the inevitable. I was compelled to end this charade of a marriage with a husband that cheated repeatedly.

The first sighting of this problem came three months after we were married when an old girlfriend called while he happened to be at his parent's home. His informing her that he was married did not deter her pursuit. So, he found ways to include her in our marriage without my permission. The birth of my first son was not the only surprise I received in the early months of 1975, I also found the phone number of my husband's chick on the side. Several signs had caused me to become suspicious and I began to investigate my hunches. I would have given anything to be wrong. I didn't want my world of security to end. We had just bought our first house, we were tucking our children into their own beds and life was looking up. I contemplated calling that number until finally I had to know. *She* did not answer the phone, but her sister did. After telling her that I found the number and was wondering who it belonged to, she said, "I was waiting for you to call." I was confused! "Why were you waiting for me to call?' "I knew you would eventually find out, and I had been telling my sister she was wrong."

Boom! Down goes Mary! My world crumbled! Not yet nineteen years old, mother of a 2 year old and a 1 month old, and now the wife of a cheating husband. I was humiliated, embarrassed, and lost with no one to turn to. I couldn't call anyone! The feelings of abandonment had crept into my life once again. Before that day, I felt I was safe. I didn't ask him to marry me, in fact, I resisted the suggestion from his mother when she told him to marry me when I was first pregnant. I didn't want a shotgun wedding. I was strong enough to go through it without a ring. So there was no need for the proposal if he wasn't ready to forsake all. He had moved to California, which was his life's dream, but decided he missed me and the baby so much, he came back home. He came back to me! To destroy my life?

It took a lot of effort to stay married without trust. I was suspicious of his every move after learning he did not have eyes for only me. I wasn't some nineteen year old college student dealing with a heartbreak, I was a nineteen year old wife. Without any spiritual guidance, we survived our days of me constantly reminding him of my unwarranted pain. I viewed everything he told me with skepticism and his touches were repulsive. I became like the green-eyed monster inspecting every move with a fine tooth comb.

With time came healing. I began to lower my defensives and life seemed to have returned to normal again. We had another son and bought another house. We had cars, money in the bank, and dreams. Suddenly, without warning, I was blind-sided. My life was tossed into a whirlwind of infidelity, again!

Old Folk's Advice

"Look the other way," was the advice an elder gave me. "All men cheat," she explained. "As long as he's taking care of you and those children and coming home like he should, look the other way."

I couldn't look the other way and pretend it wasn't happening. He had a problem and his weakness felt like an assault on my life. He was succumbing to temptations and I was living with an onslaught of feelings that were constantly present every waking moment of my life. My emotions were in a tug of war between love and hate. One moment I felt a rage and anger that fueled a sense of revenge; the next minute, I wanted to try to find common ground to repair the breach of contract for the sake of our children. The void of my father in my life was a factor in my efforts to try to press through.

    A heart can be abused so much that you begin to identify with your elements. I wrestled with taking on a new commandment of doing unto others as they did unto me. I was letting my circumstances dictate to me all over again, looking for love in all the wrong places. Eventually, I settled that I could not allow myself to become someone I'm not. On the other hand, I could not accept unwelcome affairs as a way of life and I could not stand by and see myself being a "kept" woman. The devil uses financial security as a vehicle to keep wives in marriages after extramarital affairs have been exposed. Sorrowfully, I have looked into the eyes of elderly women who have lived their lives in acceptance, with great sadness. Some wives survived the scandals of being pregnant in their family home while the other woman is pregnant with her husband's child on the next street over. The evidence left by the trail of tears were proof that sometimes looking the other way cost them more than they bargained for.

I sacrificed ten years of my life trying to live through his many indiscretions. I tried to believe him when he said he really did love me. I tried to believe him when he said he wanted our marriage to work. I didn't believe him when he said he had changed. Multiple affairs later proved me right.

A New Beginning

The night he left, two days before Valentine's Day, was the beginning of a new life for me. The separating of our lives did not happen easily. In all those years he had only damaged my soul, but now since I would not reconcile, he threatened to physically hurt me to prevent another man from having me. Life is strange, he didn't want to respect me or our marriage vows, but he didn't want me to have a chance at happiness with anyone else either. The devil was busy removing all positive male figures from my life. To succeed, satan would try to put me in the grave, my husband in jail, and my children in an orphanage. Neither the threat of bodily harm or death was enough to sway me back into that pit of hell again. I stood my ground, even while staring at the end of that rifle's barrel. I was determined to get out of that marriage, one way or another.

The pounding of a judge's gavel had taken a second man from my life; and this time, my children were abandoned also. I didn't need to read a book to learn how to survive without a man, life had taught me that. I just had to face the truth that I was in this all by myself. Nevertheless, I was determined that my children would always feel comfort in knowing that I had their backs. The devil's plan to destroy another household by removing the male as the head, had worked. But unlike my parents, I had a plan. My plan was to not only guard my children's hearts, but to also break this generational curse of absentee fathers. My new beginning in 1980 of a life with Jesus Christ had begun to prepare me how to teach my sons and my daughter to commit all things to God, making it more difficult to just walk away when things got tough.

Therefore we make it our aim, whether present or absent, to be well pleasing with Him. II Corinthians 5:9

I had to be a strong force by demonstrating godliness in deeds and not just repeating a Sunday morning cliche`. I knew God would continue to give me the wisdom to illustrate that our word is our bond, and that the greatest compliment to a human's integrity, is that he honors his word.

The world is unprincipled. It's dog-eat-dog out there! The world doesn't fight fair. But we don't live or fight our battles that way —never have and never will. The tools of our trade aren't for marketing or manipulation, but they are for demolishing that entire massively corrupt culture. We use our powerful God-tools for smashing warped philosophies, tearing down barriers erected against the truth of God, fitting every loose thought and emotion and impulse into the structure of life shaped by Christ. ..
II Corinthians 10:3-5 MSG

I was in a war. At times I wanted to crumble, rather than fight; it wasn't easy to not give up, but it was necessary for my well being as well as my children.

IT AIN'T EASY, BUT IT'S NECESSARY
Chapter Five
A Time to Heal

Resolution always brings relief, but under most circumstances, it's the hidden things that destroy us.

Wherever there's divorce, there's changes in patterns. There's more room in the garage, more room in the closet, one less toothbrush in the holder, one less place setting on the table, tons of questions and lots of *"what ifs."* While the official seal on the decree finalizes the seen, the unseen waits on the sideline unattended. *Was something wrong with me? Why wasn't I enough? What did she have that I didn't? Why am I so unlovable?*

Through much soul searching, I've learned that when someone cheats it's not because of something I did or did not do, it's their choice. Could I have been a better wife? Maybe. Could I have been picture perfect? Possibly. Would that have made a difference in his choice? No!

The temptation to give in to evil comes from us and only us. We have no one to blame but the leering, seducing flare-up of our own lust. Lust gets pregnant, and has a baby: sin! Sin grows up to adulthood, and becomes a real killer. James 1:14-15 (MSG)

Nothing in my power existed that could have prevented my husband's decision to be unfaithful. It was a seed of iniquity that had grown in him that made him believe all men cheat and wives should look the other way. I truly believe that his intentions to live happily ever after were sincere, but there's power in words. Proverbs 18:21 tells us that life and death is in the power of the tongue. If the words "adultery is a serious offense in the eyes of God and it should not be taken lightly" were planted, instead of "all men cheat", I'm sure the results would have been different. Evidence of the AIDS epidemic's continual growth proves that our conscience can become so seared that we risk life and death to satisfy our flesh.

I had been divorced for eight years and had remarried when suddenly the Spirit of God began to say, "Mary, you're bitter." The conversation continued in this fashion: "About what God?" "Your ex-husband," He replied. "No, I'm not," was my response because honestly I felt that the declaration of divorce had fixed everything. Obviously, the Holy Spirit knew I <u>had not dealt with the affects that betrayal causes</u>, so He persisted twice more until I surrendered. The Spirit of God revealed to me that every time my ex's name came through my thought channels, I became angry. I was guilty as charged. I would begin reenacting familiar scenes, only this time I would change the endings where I am always violently hurting my ex-husband.

I protested that I had a right to be angry because of all I had endured. I not only dreamed of hurting him, but whenever asked, I told all my unsuspecting friends about the nightmare I had lived through those ten years. Being able to degrade him in any way was my trophy. Sounds foolish, but it was like mounting the head of a deer, it was my visual testimony that I had subdued. As the Holy Spirit continued to gently minister to me, He spoke, "You have a reason for being angry, but as a child of God, you gave up your *rights to be angry*." "On the cross," he went on, "Jesus paid the price for every sin known to man by the shedding of His blood. That blood sacrifice presented to God, the Father, erased all condemnation against the human race. God forgave, and being Christ like, you must forgive also." Again, I argued, "How do I forgive someone who so recklessly destroyed my life?" Shockingly, He said, "Pray for him." "Pray for him," I asked? "Every time the devil brings him into your mind, pray for him," He urged.

Eventually, I went on to tell the Holy Spirit that I would do as instructed and pray for him, but I would not pray some long drawn out prayer that I did not mean. From that point forward, every time his name came into my mind, I would simply pray, "Save him." As much as I hated him, I was not so cold hearted that I would wish hell on anyone, so I sincerely prayed, "Save him." The effects were not instant. It took me taking a firm stand against the devil whenever he tried to fill my mind with reasons for hating, and to my amazement, I found the rage that I once entertained upon hearing his name, subsiding. Of course, the devil had no desire for me to send up prayers on my ex-husband's behalf, so he stopped tormenting me with the injustices with which he had infested my life. Throughout this whole process, I learned to forgive my enemies, and gained peace of mind.

Initially, I was unaware that bitterness was holding me hostage for someone else's crime. The works of the flesh, if allowed to sit in the control seat, will only bring hurtful, damaging, and even deadly results to the lives of the guilty and the innocent. If our flesh is left unchecked, it will manifest desires that makes it feel good at any cost. Like a ninety mile per hour wind, satan, using the flesh, will kill, steal, and destroy anything in its path to get what it wants.

It is obvious what kind of life develops out of trying to get your own way all the time: repetitive, loveless, cheap sex; a stinking accumulation of mental and emotional garbage; frenzied and joyless grabs for happiness; trinket gods; magic-show religion; paranoid loneliness; cutthroat competition; all-consuming-yet-never-satisfied wants; a brutal temper; an impotence to love or be loved; divided homes and divided lives; small-minded and lopsided pursuits; the vicious habit of depersonalizing everyone into a rival; uncontrolled and uncontrollable addictions; ugly parodies of community Galatians 5:19 (MSG)

    Leaving his unclean thoughts unbridled, my ex's thinking turned into actions of adultery. In my case, after the dust had settled, I revisited my past often and the resentment began to build. My attention was also on uncontrolled lewd and unclean thoughts. My heart was wounded and any wrong turn could have sparked a fit of rage, turning my thoughts into unclean actions. The Holy Spirit rescued me from the road map the devil was devising to bring about destruction. Thank God that I stood in submission to the Light when He revealed my darkness. It's not easy giving up ones right to hatred, but it's necessary for the sake of being Christ-like.

IT AIN'T EASY, BUT IT'S NECESSARY
Chapter Six
At the Feet of Jesus

My entire life had been centered around going to Sunday School and Church on Sunday mornings and BTU (Baptist Training Union) on Sunday evenings, followed by evening services. Saturday mornings were set aside for youth choir practices and when the seasons dictated, Easter and Christmas play rehearsals. I can truly say, that I loved the Lord. As a child, I remember the closeness I experienced as I sang *Blessed Assurance, Jesus is Mine*. There was an unspoken knowing within, that He was always near.

A lot of the traditions of our Baptist Covenant were illustrated in honor to a building, which I found strange. You couldn't take a shortcut across the pulpit, only the sacred feet of ministers treaded there. The forbidding of lying in church or lying on a Sunday was also a rule that was greatly emphasized. People would walk across the street from the church to smoke, but never on the campus. If someone did commit a sin, it was never spoken of in the church's sanctuary, only in the whispers of your homes away from the ears of the children.

Never Late

Somewhere in the midst of all those regiments I still had a longing to please God. It was no wonder when in June of 1980 at the declaration of a dear friend saying, "I got saved last night," I felt jealousy. She went on to explain that I might not believe her, but I did. I knew there was something else to God than where I should place my feet or what words I should say on what day. Being such a new babe in Christ left her only armed with the words, "I asked Him to come into my heart."

My heart churned all day as I needed to say what she said, I needed to meet the Jesus she had met. I knew Him, but I didn't. He was the One I knew was always near, the One whose presence I sensed. It was as if my day was orchestrated by God. I hurried home, alone for some reason, without picking up the kids. I frantically ran from room to room as if I expected to see Jesus sitting there waiting on me. I picked up the phone in an effort to call a lady that talked differently from the other church women, but her line was busy. In a last ditched effort, I fell on my knees and simply said, "Jesus, I don't know what to say, but I know I want what Barbara has. Please come into my heart too." As tears began to stream down my face, I knew that He was there. I knew that I had an encounter with God and my life would never be the same.

For God so loved the world that He gave His only begotten Son, that whoever believes in Him should not perish but have everlasting life. For God did not send His Son into the world to condemn the world, but that the world through Him might be saved. John 3:16-17 (NKJV)

Hey world, I got saved!

I picked up my Bible and began to read. Nothing in particular, just reading. I was ecstatic. I was singing, I was reading, I was with Jesus. When the doors of my home flew open and my husband and the children came in, I unleashed all my excitement onto him. I got saved today. Nothing! (crickets) Why isn't he smiling? Why isn't he excitedly rejoicing with me? Talk about a party pooper. All the air went out of my balloons as Barbara's other words returned to my memory, "I know you might not believe me."

I couldn't wait to get to work the next morning so I could tell someone about my new birth that would understand. A righteous jealousy opened a new world to me. "Barbara, I got saved last night."

Hope

Hearing about Jesus stirred a hope in me and brought relief from a suffocating feeling that life in the real world was not worth participating in. The years I spent locked in my room listening to recordings about love, heartache, joy, and devastation, had paved an imaginary tunnel of escape that separated me from reality. Whenever my existence in the real world became chaotic, I would disappear into an intangible world where I was in control. This way of escape was comforting, but yet dangerous; and at the time I didn't know it!

It was not of God, it was not His way of escape for me. It was me clawing for any form of survival I could find and music opened up a suggestive form of freedom that allowed me to enter a world mentally that didn't require my physical presence. It didn't have to actually be real, just real to me. However, this way of escape separated me from the holy God I served because He is a God of truth. As

John 8:32 states, truth sets you free! I was in trouble and didn't know it. But God...who's never too late, knew that now was the time for there was a trap set for me that was hidden like a bear trap buried beneath the leaves.

Perfect

In my pretend world I had a perfect family, that consisted of a perfect husband who adored me. I gave him perfect babies and whenever I decided to let disappointment in, my suddenly flawed husband would turn the world upside down to win my devotion again.

Having spent so many years in secret sadness, building a safe fortress, even though it was imaginary, was creating a barrier that was not built on truth. I was emotionally attached so deeply to my secret family that I resented any disturbances brought on by reality. I would promptly tend to realism only to hastily return to my make believe world. Every move I made was for the household within. I grocery shopped mimicking it was for them, I washed *their* clothes. The impersonators within my secured world had taken over my soul. It had become a stronghold that had taken me captive, unknowingly, I was in bondage. This world that existed only in my mind was a part of my life, my heart, for years.

Psychotic

It's strange how we are created. We hate the life we live, but instinctively we fight to survive. As far back as I can remember, I have always had a creative ability to write screens of hope in my life. At the age of four or five, I remember having a vivid life in my room with my dollhouse, dolls, and tea sets. They weren't plastic and wood, they were my family. I belonged there, I was welcomed. I was unknowingly surviving. I was not psychotic, just a wounded soul looking for a way to escape the script of *my* life; and like a drowning victim, I was struggling to reach the surface for air.

While watching a movie about a man who had been institutionalized for five years for killing his wife and two daughters, a floodgate opened. I saw myself in the character that the actor played. The judiciary system had no concrete proof that he was the killer so they committed him to a mental hospital where he struggled to free himself from his true identity, from the branded label of murderer. On the outside, he looked the same, but within his soul, in that secret passage that no one can invade unless invited, he slipped into his life as he envisioned it to be before the tragedy under a new name.

Armed only with assumptions, the courts were obligated to release him once he was declared fit to live in society. Upon his release, in his efforts to break free from the cruel false accusations that he had murdered his family, he internalized his grief by pretending they were not dead, but still home with him. Everything he did involved him making a perfect home life for them.

I was not accused of a crime or institutionalized, but that was me. The emotional and mental neglect had driven me into a world of make believe in order to cope with the ugliness that may seem so minor to others, yet so devastating to me. I was lost, wandering, looking for something, anything, to make sense.

One evening, while desperately needing to escape the turmoil of my failing marriage, I secretly snuck away into the channel of my unblemished pretend life. While there, in reality, I fell asleep. I was unaware that I had meditated myself to a point where I had literally lost control of my soul. I was spinning through the atmosphere of stars and planets headed somewhere. I wasn't afraid, I had no fear of falling or heights. I didn't see anyone else, I was just traveling...to somewhere. Suddenly, the Holy Spirit used the ringing of the telephone to bring me out of my slumber. Hearing the ringing, I began to attempt to get up to answer the call. I was literally in the twilight zone. As I fought to regain my composure, I was spinning back through darkness with shooting lights flashing all around me. I stood on my feet and stumbled for the phone, but the Deceiver was restricting me. It was not my eyesight but my memory that got me to that phone. I could not see, my hearing and feeling were back to earth, but my eyes only saw darkness and my mind was filled with confusion. I don't have words to describe what I was going through, but I know I was caught between two worlds. As I picked up the receiver, unable to talk, it was my mother's human voice shouting, "Mary," repeatedly that broke the power that obscured my complete return to actuality.

    Still unstable, it took a few minutes to clear my head. My episode was an experience I would envision a person on LSD having. Not realizing how much trouble I was in, the Holy Spirit began to explain to me that I had meditated myself out of my body and was being snatched into darkness. He showed me that my pretend world was constructed on lies and the fortress it created only manufactured a temporary relief, but did nothing to solve any problems. I was doing exactly what Proverbs 3:5,6 taught me not to do, leaning to my own strengths and not letting God direct my path. The Bible teaches us to meditate, but on truth, on the Word of God, not on fake pretense. It was all designed by the Deceiver to blind me from the facts that life hurts and there's no denying it. The escape route that the meditation gave me almost cost me my life. It was the same practice as chanting in front of a buddhist statue. Nothing is fixed, you just learn to channel your energy away from the anger, away from the pain. God showed me that *He is my refuge and my fortress. It is in Him that I should put my trust in.* (Proverbs 91:2).

Back to Reality

Coming out of meditation into God's arms was like walking through a heavily wooded forest. I knew that I wanted to go home, but the trip there proved more challenging than I expected. The issues in my life that led me to this place of deceit came from a combination of hurts throughout my life, each stemming from being disappointed with love. The disconnect from my parents, my family; the disappointment of my husband giving his attention, his touch, his time to other women all led to me making sadness a continual chaperon of my life. However, I did not stand in that forest alone, the Holy Spirit was my constant companion. My only requirement was to give Him my hand, which signified a willing heart that wanted to be led out, and not look back. There was no doubt of my willingness, it was my flesh, however, that was weak.

Watch and pray, lest you enter into temptation. The spirit indeed is willing, but the flesh is weak. Matthew 26:41

I had lived in that place of contentment for so long and never realized I was in any danger. As silly as it sounds, it was a struggle letting go of *my family*. My world was fabricated, but to a person so starved for acceptance and appreciation, it was safe. My Comforter was asking me to let that bogus activity incinerate and return to a place of vulnerability where love does hurt. I was so afraid. I was not being promised that I would never experience hurt again. There was no written agreement that I would never feel let down, beat down, or unimportant. All the things my enchanted forest offered were being reduced to ashes. It was erected on lies and I had to let it fall before it destroyed me.

But when I am afraid, I will put my trust in you. I praise God for what he has promised. I trust in God, so why should I be afraid? What can mere mortals do to me? Psalm 56:3,4 (NLT)

Thank God for redemption that comes with longsuffering and kindness, for I looked back at and actually visited my man made haven several times for months before I became strong enough to walk away. It was my continual study of the Word that broke the spell. The pleasure of my visits into the world of make believe were less satisfying as I put my trust in God's promises. It was not an easy encounter because the Deceiver fought mightily to keep me in restraints. The ugliness of life did not disappear and the fight to not take matters into my own hands was a horrific battle. Nevertheless, it was necessary that I face real life head on in order to save myself from an early grave or a psychiatric institution.

How many people, I wonder, are in their graves now or branded with some psychotic diagnosis, such as schizophrenia, who are really just those who were struggling to survive and missed the hand God offered to help. *Dear God, I pray, that Truth prevails.*

IT AIN'T EASY BUT IT'S NECESSARY
Chapter Seven
God, I Quit

Like all little girls playing with their dolls and tea sets, I formed an idea of what I wanted my life to be like. However, circumstances altered my plans, so as a teenager, I determined I wanted all sons, no daughters.

On top of all the other struggles I had in my life, I was saddled with excruciatingly painful and heavy menstrual cycles. As a preteen, I felt cursed since, from day one, my tummy ached. A few years of curling up with heating pads and *tossing my cookies* persuaded me that no girl child deserved to live life this way. This birthed my declaration for *no girls*.

As fate would have it, my first born was a girl. It's true you forget all the silliness stored in your head when you see her for the first time. I didn't think about some ungrateful man breaking her heart or painful cycles, I only promised her I would do all I could to make her world special.

Choosing to do all the right things, I dressed her in the frilly little dresses, rompers, and socks, followed by matching hair bows. I attended musical recitals, soccer games, church dramas, track meets, and basketball games; the works. I wasn't perfect, but I was always present.

Then, she developed into a teenager. In came the clothes, different hair styles, boyfriends, and plenty of attitude. Years later, hindsight showed me that hidden behind the attitude was a silent animosity against her dad and a member of his family. She was not disturbed by the divorce, she was hurt that he left her and her brothers. Sadly, her dad remained true to his word that if I divorced him, he would divorce them. With him being absent, I became the target of her fury. Hurting people do hurt people, and it's often the closest one available. If I said it was up, she said down. If I said stop, she would go. If there was peace, she became like a whirlwind stirring up confusion. Her younger brothers were also the victims of her rage. She would bully them because she was the oldest. There were no signs that led me to believe she even had her dad on her mind. She didn't make any attempts, to my knowledge, to seek him out so I was clueless about how to correct her irritation. No amount of punishments alleviated the situations for long.

Right before her high school graduation, mentally exhausted, I said in my heart, "God, I quit." I was hopeless and helpless when it came to bringing some sort of resolution to my relationship with my daughter. The only light I saw at the end of this tunnel was after she graduated she would soon be off to her next phase of life. God whispered, "I'll take her then." "Take her, what do you mean take her?" I challenged! "This is her best time to make it to heaven, so I'll take her," God replied. "No God, I don't want my little girl to die, I just want her to be happy for once." "Mary," God spoke in a quiet voice, "If a *mother* won't fight for her child, who will?" "God," I cried, "I don't know what to do, she fights me at every turn. Even when we go to church, she's mad." He instructed, "Satan wants you to stop praying for your child so she will be uncovered. He's trying to make you give up on her so her hedge of protection would be removed. If you don't pray, she will be naked and exposed to all kinds of evil."

    I wasn't quitting because I didn't love my daughter, I just wanted the discord to end. All the topsy-turviness was keeping us arms length apart. I wanted to embrace her, to enjoy her, to celebrate her. She was my first born. She had been with me the longest and we had grown up together. The option of losing my child gave me the strength to retrieve the white flag and fight on. I wanted her to live a full life with all the promises God had for her, so back to my knees I went.

18 Years Later

God knew the pain she suffered even though it was still concealed from me. Eventually, after reconnecting with her dad in 2009, it came out.

During some down time in her life after surgery, my daughter and I spent more time together talking. She began to reveal an aunt's mistreatment of her. The aunt took advantage of my daughter's youth and would hit her. I did not realize the severity of this misconduct and I asked her why she didn't inform me? She said that she made it known to her dad, but he did nothing about it. As a woman of God, I kept my composure and prayed, but as a mother, in my mind, I balled up my fist. I pondered my mind for signs I could have missed. I questioned my allowing this person to be a caregiver for my children as I worked. Had my daughter reached out to me and I failed to protect her? I know she didn't like to visit my in-laws, but I couldn't rightfully deny her visits when her dad took her with him. No mother wants to feel as if she failed her child, but maybe God was preventing me from having a criminal charge on my profile.

It's unfortunate that even years later my daughter was unable to form a relationship with her dad. Her efforts to be a part of his world were unfruitful. As she tried, I had to sit back and wait for the outcome. I prayed that the years had brought about a change and for her sake, the reconciliation would be possible.

I took my daughter back to the year of 1992 when God told me to pray for her dad. Despite the painful memories, I informed her that my visit to the cross of Jesus had relieved me of all my pent-up frustrations. It was now her turn to allow the Holy Spirit to free her from the bitterness she held against her dad and her aunt. Her confession of not knowing how she would react if she ever saw that aunt again was evidence that she was imprisoned by her anger.

All the substitutions of love in the world cannot usurp God's place as Supreme Love. We look for love in the faces and places of people who are damaged. Truthfully, no human will ever escape the wrath of sin, and love is doomed to be flawed through mankind. As hard as I tried to steer my children from the pain I went through, sin still highjacked my plans. I was flawed, their dad was flawed, their destination was fated toward destruction unless routed through God. Even then, we must accept that only God's love is pure and untainted, and we will never experience it in it's immaculate form until we are free from this earth.

    As I write, my heart's cry is for my sons to be freed from an unspoken indignation toward their dad. They just won't talk about him. Their children have no idea that "Papa" is not their biological grandfather. While my husband has been an exceptional father to my children and their dad deserves no rightful place in our lives, truth cannot be concealed. He was not the one who cheered for you, he was not the one who you could depend on, but when anger keeps you from acknowledging who he is, then there's a problem.

    In the process of separating our lives, while dealing with their father's pointless attempts to reconcile, my oldest son stepped in when his dad's anger took things too far. He was only nine years old, but I still remember his small hand grabbing his dad's wrist as he told him to take his hands off his mother. His courage brought my little David face to face with Goliath. I can still envision his face with his scrunched brow and flaring nostrils. He didn't take time to consider the ramification of his actions, so with as much authority as a nine year old can muster, he stared into the eyes of his dad one last time and something died.

My youngest son, then seven, was the baby. He was his father's side-kick so I'm not sure what he experienced during that time. However, as years passed and he grew into a young man, I have seen him on two occasions become the bigger man by extending his hand to his dad. Both times he left shaking his head, with the latter being the final blow. Once again, something died.

Whether it's a secret bond or an unspoken truth, the two boys, share a wound that needs healing. I know God has a plan for some laborer to cross their path one day, someone who will be able, with the grace of God, to touch those wounds and bring them out of hiding. For it is in the Light that we heal, darkness allows that which is hidden in secret to fester and grow.

For I know the plans I have for you," says the Lord. "They are plans for good and not for disaster, to give you a future and a hope. Jeremiah 29:11 (NLT)

As my son once protected me so long ago, I must fight through prayer to protect them both. They, nor their sister, are responsible for being birthed into utter confusion because I didn't have the spiritual knowledge to take everything to God in prayer first. I based love on feelings not realizing that it should have been based on commitment. I didn't examine his beliefs or his goals. The price I paid cost me more than I could afford, but I promise to the remaining three treasures, my beautiful babies, that I will show them the way to put God first in all their decisions so that their crooked places will be made straight. It's hard to know your babies are hurting and you are helpless within yourself to fix things, but it's necessary to not give up and keep trusting God for a better day.

IT AIN'T EASY, BUT IT'S NECESSARY
Chapter Eight
I AM LOVE

Love is so amazing

Everyone has pulled that extra pillow into their arms as they drifted to sleep dreaming of the day when that bundle of foam would become flesh, alive and vibrant, and yours. You would no longer have to use your imagination of being wanted, loved, and desired, but it would finally become a reality.

Love is magical

It begins with your eyes and penetrates your heart so deeply that you can't imagine spending a day of your life without that special one that you call yours. Your soul becomes so entangled that they are on your mind constantly and your only desire is to be with them. Even a song over the speakers at the grocery store can send you floating down the aisles as you are emotionally swept away into the arms of your love as their piercing eyes see you as no other can. As others pass you, smiles radiate as they recognize that look on your face that they once wore on theirs. You will even high five a total stranger as your heart testifies to the memories that once weakened your knees and poured joy into your atmosphere.

Love is mystical

It is something that begins in the innermost depth of your soul and radiates out through your five senses. A touch of your hand feels like no other touch, and that look; the look that's shared between the two of you that sends those electrical vibes that triggers your brain to pull up the file that's labeled for just the two of you. Love is so mysterious that moments shared have caused us to speak praises to our God for the blessings that He has bestowed upon us only to be quickly followed by embarrassment as we blush at the thought of our Heavenly Father knowing we have experienced such pleasure. Love touches that part of us that we can't rub with a salve when it's throbbing or even be satisfied with the greatest lover known to mankind, if that lover is a substitute.

Loving that special one has taken us to such heights that we are able to stand on the highest mountain. But even the highest mountains have storms. It is during that time, when the thunderous storms are drowning out the melody of your favorite song, that you must decide to stand. It's when you look into the eyes of your love and don't see "you" anymore that you must decide that all those blessings that once made you praise the name of the Lord are worth fighting for.

A Journey in Wisdom

After going through a heart wrenching marriage that inevitably ended in divorce, a messenger of God was sent to bring me a book that was entitled, *"Hinds Feet on High Places"*, by Hannah Hurnard. The book was beautifully written as it described its main character *Much Afraid's* journey to the higher places. However, along her path were many obstacles and schemes of the enemy to prevent her from reaching the greatest reward that awaited her at the assigned destination, Eternity.

Immediately, I was able to place my feet into the shoes of this character, as I too was so afraid of ever loving again. Scars remained so deeply embedded in my soul that it made me cringe to even think of trusting another with my heart. Thoughts of the many infidelities shook my confidence in being a woman capable of being loved.

Especially, as memories flooded my mind with the lies that were told to cover the stolen minutes that were promised to me and me alone during our ceremony before God and man. My love's heart's intentions were pledged to me until death do we part but something swayed him into finding pleasure in the scent of another's perfume as she laid in the arms that were meant for me only.

I didn't realize that as I sat reading, I was about to begin my own journey of repairing the ruins of my life. As the Holy Spirit patiently chiseled at my self-imposed walls of protection which I used as a barrier to keep others out, He knew, unbeknownst to me, they also kept me locked in.

Love makes one vulnerable

There came a time I called a halt to the chiseling because the last thing I wanted to hear was that in order to love someone I must willingly allow myself to be vulnerable. To place my heart into someone's hands, meant that he had the power to hurt me. Isn't that what caused me to move into this fortress of self protection in the first place? It was at that moment that I discovered that God had a sense of humor...but I wasn't laughing. Tears still well up in my eyes as I remember asking my Father how He could ask me to love anyone so freely again that they could literally take me back to the very place that I ran to get far away from with great haste. There were no memories left of that mystical, mysterious, and magical love. It had been replaced with deceit, followed by resentment and bitterness, and finally sealed with hatred. My dreams of being in his arms were gone, replaced by thoughts of driving an ice pick through his ear as he slept, wondering if it would pierce his brain. I couldn't remember our songs anymore because hearing them brought tears of sadness as I remembered the way we once were but were no longer, because he decided to taste forbidden fruit.

    It's strange, that even today when I hear a train's whistle in the early morning hours, it takes me back to the sleepless nights because of a battled and wounded heart that allowed no rest for the weary. "Lord," I prayed, "I'm okay right here in my protected cocoon. I don't need a man to be all he won't be to me. I can do bad by myself and I choose not to let all that chaos into my world." What I didn't realize was that God was not trying to chisel an opening for a man, He wanted one for Himself.

    It had been five years since I had given my life to God but yet, He was inviting me to take a closer look to learn the truth of His love. I thought that God was instructing me to become vulnerable to a man when actually His invitation was more personal; become vulnerable to Him. Peeping through a crack between the door and it's facings, not brave enough to open it, I saw the scriptures that said we must love those that persecute us, love those that despitefully use us, love those incarcerated, love those that are poor, love those that are unlovable...

I hurled that book so far under my bed because now God was asking too much. I can love the incarcerated, I can love the poor, but you were stretching me too far out of my comfort zone when you asked me to love the people that took my heart into their hands and annihilated it like meat in a meat grinder. "You, Daddy, want me to love those that treated me disrespectfully... as if I didn't matter? How do you love hate, because that's what I felt, hated. Mean spirited people live in their own worlds and the only time they step outside of it is when they get caught. Then comes the water works, along with the lame apologies. How do you love the unlovable that display not an ounce of godliness, and why?" "Because I do," replied the Lord. "I shed my blood for all mankind because they were all born into sin because of Adam. I don't measure sin, it's all stench in my nostrils. A person who murders one with words is in just as much need of cleansing as a person who murders one with a gun or knife. My blood cleanses all that it touches." I knew that God was able to love in spite of a person's deeds, He's God. I just questioned how He expected me to love His way, too.

From the time of purchase, to slinging it under the bed, to finally crawling under the bed to retrieve the book again from it's trap of dust bunnies, almost four years had gone by. My heart had only grown more frigid toward love as I spent four years dodging God's appeal to talk to Him.

Talk to Me

With two pre-teens and a teenager in the house, I often found a quiet haven sitting outside on my car. I would marvel at the moon and the stars or the lack thereof. God's creation was breathtaking. Who could doubt that a Superior Power, one who could make something out of nothing, existed? Years earlier, I had spent many hours talking with God there. Despite our discord on love, I would still wander there, it was peaceful.

"Mary, talk to Me," His Voice was gentle and I was relieved that He still desired to talk with me. "No," I responded! "Mary," 'No, God,' I interrupted. 'You only want me to hurt. I love You, but I don't like the way you ask me to let others hurt me." "Talk to Me," He whispered. Shaking my head "no," I left my haven but stopped to look back as if I could see Him there. I wanted to talk, but I just didn't want to hurt and I knew His love offered no such guarantees. So I remained quiet.

The World's Love

The years I spent running from God and His teachings on vulnerable love, left me gullible and exposed, as I played in the cesspool of sin. I had loved right and was hurt, now all bets were off and I was taking my life into my own hands. Tina Turner's record, *"What's Love Got to Do With It,"* had hit the world. She was taking her life back from her abusive husband and I wanted to ride. My new anthem freed me from that complicated action of love. Let's have fun. New rules: Don't love me because I promise, I won't love you. Men laughed at me as if a woman was incapable of not loving. They didn't know my secret though, I had a fortress that was foolproof and built on pain. I had mentally checked out and no man would ever hurt me again. I had heard enough lies and experienced enough disappointments to last me a lifetime.

It felt good to not answer a call. I wasn't worried that he wouldn't call back, I didn't care! I lived by my own rules and danced to the beat of my own drum. What's love got to do with it? My only commitment was to my children. They were the ones I clung to, anyone else was on a take it or leave it basis.

Truth be told, I soon tired of that lifestyle, too. It had its ups, but it was also empty and meaningless. I wasn't being someone's puppet but I couldn't keep my eyes off the hill where true joy existed. I was a prodigal daughter, not wasting my means, but squandering my time, and I missed my Father. I had backslidden from my true love, God; and I missed being in fellowship. I wished someone would have thrown me a lifeline. I was smiling on the outside, but inwardly, I wanted to go home.

As if accepting the offer of the angel, I came out of Egypt, but I didn't go home. I wanted God to meet me on my terms, offer me love without pain. Give me a promise that He would't let people persecute me. "Protect me please, Daddy! I just want to feel safe and loved."

I began to live my life man-free and I loved it. Once again, I was at peace. I gave my undivided attention to my growing children with no distractions. Months had passed when a phone call from my cousin shattered my self made world. "Cous, when are you going to get married again," she asked innocently, to which I replied, "Girl, what's love got to do with it?" Suddenly, in the center of my being, I heard the voice of God say very loudly, "Love has everything to do with it, I AM LOVE!" I looked around to see if maybe God was standing there, the Voice was just that real. I told my cousin I would have to call her back, as I backed into the corner of my room trying to explain to God, I didn't mean it like that. "I'm sorry, Dad, but why does Your love hurt," I asked? His words were simple, "Get the book." He had orchestrated the delivery of that book to me for a purpose. He knew my heart was wounded by man so He wanted to teach me about His love. No, He couldn't guarantee that I wouldn't get hurt again, in fact, He promised I would, because life in its sinful state, was full of disappointments. His promise was, that as I went through the certified hardships, He would be right there to go through them with me, lessening the pain.

  My journey of reading that book was delayed for four years by fear. I confess, I winced through many of the pages, as Much Afraid's adventure was hindered by bitterness, resentment, fear, discouragement, and any other negative force the Deceiver could throw at her. I cheered though, as Jesus always came to her rescue. His assurance was, "just call Me, I'll always come," and He did, sometimes not as fast as she wanted, but always. The things Much Afraid suffered might have bent her a little, maybe at times a lot, but she never broke. The Good Shepherd was always true to His Word.

Upon the completion of *Hinds Feet on High Places*, I was faced with the question, Is Jesus enough? Is Jesus enough when someone breaks your heart or when the news is cancer? Is He enough when your dreams and hopes don't materialize or when the money is not there? Is Jesus enough that you will accept His goodness and His sufferings?

Though He was a Son, yet He learned obedience by the things which He suffered Hebrews 5:8 (NKJ)

The word suffering makes me back up. No one enjoys pain. However, if I'm to be like Jesus, then I'll suffer. I'll suffer because this world won't like that I choose holiness and I choose to stand against unholiness. I'll suffer because the Deceiver will do all that he can to stop my voice from delivering the message that Jesus saves and delivers. As the darkness of this world continues to increase on the television screens and in the lyrics of some of the most foul music known to man, I will not succumb to the pressure to be counted among the popular; therefore, I will be shunned. I won't be liked because I will change my channels, remove my presence, refuse to buy, refuse to indulge. As I refuse to stamp "ok" on all that the world says is "your thang, do what you want to do," I will be unfriended, and ostracized. Throughout the ruggedness of my pilgrimage, I will be faced daily with the question, "Is Jesus enough?" In good times and bad times? Yes! In sickness and in health? Yes! Through richness and poverty? Yes! Till death or rapture departs your soul from this earth? Yes, Jesus is enough!

IT AIN'T EASY, BUT IT'S NECESSARY
Chapter Nine
Love is Kind

If you think that you've learned all you need to know just because your salvation birth date has double digits, think again. I had a close encounter with Jesus in June of 1980 and here I sit 35 years later in the classroom of the famous chapter, I Corinthians 13.

Have you ever had days in your marriage where you didn't want to leave, but you didn't want to stay either? Days when you needed to dwell in your very own domain where only your ways mattered, where only your opinions are considered? Sometimes you just need moments where it's okay to be selfish and think only of yourself. I believe that God allows us to have those moments as long as we don't camp out there. It's like being allowed to go outside for a breath of fresh air before you *continue*.

God's kind of love does everything but self serve. It's an inward love that outwardly gives to others. It's a love that loves regardless of the return. It's a love that promises to still exist even if you choose to make your bed in hell. God's love comes with no ultimatums, no limits, no ifs. He just loves.

Love is kind, God is kind, God is love! His kindness is a gift!

Don't you see how wonderfully kind, tolerant, and patient God is with you? Does this mean nothing to you? Can't you see that His kindness is intended to turn you from your sin?
Romans 2:4 (NLT)

Don't continue to bring dirt into a house that's already dirty; clean it up!

Love is Kind

Love suffers long and is kind I Corinthians 13:4a

In any relationship, but especially in a marriage, what happens when your knowledge of the dos and don'ts of love grows, but your partner hasn't? Do you end your marriage because it's inevitable that the socks will never make it to the hamper? God says "No!"

Irritations, whether big or small, are weighed according to each individual's life experiences. Ten years of unrepented infidelity was the breaking point in my first marriage. Someone else might not have had the strength to tolerate it a year, while others might have had the strength to tolerate this annoyance because momma tolerated it, or because they are financially comfortable, or maybe they believed their mate would grow out of it and they were strong enough to patiently wait. There are no limits to grace. It is an endless gift from an endless God.

However, while dealing with life, grace demands that love is kind, whether it's easy or not. As Headmaster of the classroom to all who choose to attend, the Holy Spirit, inspired the writer to pen its first example of love as being longsuffering and kind. An in depth study of longsuffering showed that it endured injury, trouble, or provocation long and patiently. One of the synonyms for longsuffering is *uncomplaining*. Further study shows that the word kind was associated with seventeen strong synonyms all having to do with the giving of yourself for the betterment of others with no reference to the degree or limit to such gift.

With kindness at the forefront of any marriage, then fights, disagreements, or opinions stay within the guidelines established by God. Kindness corrals self-centeredness and evil thinking. Kindness lowers voices, softens tones, and commands respect to stand guard over our mouths. By walking in kindness, love is able to rejoice in truth while covering ones' weaknesses with prayer. Being kind is an act of love that chooses to bear all things and to believe when there is no hope. To be kind is to be cordial, courteous, decent, gentle, hospitable, affectionate, patient, understanding, and sympathetic. When I allow love to blossom from within me, I become kind. When I'm kind, I cast down evil thoughts and push envying to the side. When I was a child, I spoke as a child, I understood as a child, but now that I'm sitting in this classroom and learning about this long suffering love, how do I put away my childish feelings of wanting a limit to my sacrifices? "I know love suffers long', dear God, 'but how long is long enough?"

Through the Eyes of God

Just as a parent waits patiently for that first step of their growing toddler, so God waits patiently for us to move from one phase to the next, as He cheers us on.

Divorced, after ten years of marriage, I spent six years single before marrying again. Before saying "I do" the second time, it was only by the urging of the Holy Spirit that I even began to entertain the thought of marriage again. Having become comfortable in my life with my Brat Pack, as I affectionately called my children, I was content with enjoying my life with them. After several promptings, I surrendered my list of wants in a husband to the Holy Spirit, with all honesty, just to affectionately get Him off my back.

We have such confidence in Him that we are certain that He hears every request that is made in accord with His own plan. And since we know that He invariably gives His attention to our prayers, whatever they are about, we can be quite sure that our prayers will be answered. I John 5:14-15 (Phillips)

'He needs to love my children as his own,' was my first desire, followed by height, weight, skin complexion, and 'I should never wonder one day of my life if he loves me,' was my ending. Being a novice at this request thing, I now know that I should have extended that list to detail more matters of my heart. However, to my amazement, God gave me a husband, *that found me*, Proverbs 18:22, and fulfilled my desired requests to the tee.

In my years of training as a child, there was a very strict hand of discipline upon me to do things right the first time and get it done. Through prophecy, years later, a very dear friend of mine told me that God allowed my grandmother's stern hand upon me to get me ready for my ministry. Our household consisted of my mother, grandmother, brother and me. My grandmother took me under her wing and taught me some valuable lessons that might seem insignificant to some, but for me they turned out to be lessons of gold. I remember, at five years old, she taught me to always have a plan. While her teachings surrounded physical survival, they are still a strong staple in my life today. She taught me how to take a little and stretch it to its maximum; to fulfill my needs first, and my wants with patience. I watched her use the lay-away plan as smoothly as a well oiled wheel. We had no lack in our lives. The system would have called us poor by their standards, but others viewed us as fortunate. My grandmother made life happen, one way or another.

In the sixties, the mildness of the weather did not pressure us to have an air-conditioner, so we slept with our windows open. Living in a time where crime was unheard of did not deter my grandmother's knowledge that fools still existed, so she taught me to sleep with a hatchet under my pillow. I practiced to perfection keeping my right hand on the handle while my left hand remained tucked under me, free from injury. Her instructions were that if anyone ever tried to come through my window, don't say a word, pull the hatchet from under the pillow, and hit them right in the top of their head. Trusting in everything she taught me, I know without a doubt, if I was ever faced with such a dilemma, even at five years old, I would have executed our plan without a hitch. I was trained to have a plan.

In the list of wants I presented to the Holy Spirit concerning a husband, I failed to mention that I was a very systematic person who had a precise place for everything and everything was to be in that precise place. I had a keen sense of knowing when something had changed, but I didn't put that on my list. My new husband was far from systematic and lived a very free spirited life. He was very spontaneous, very instinctive. His plan was to live and let everything take care of itself. "God are you kidding me? Are you playing a joke on me?"

This vast difference in our way of doing things caused a lot of friction in our marriage. The cabinet doors were left opened and his shoes and socks were under the coffee table in the living room. He didn't believe it was necessary to make a bed because you were only going to get back in it later. He never put anything back in it's precise place and was never bothered by the untidy piles that were accumulating in the corner. My husband's practice of "I'm going to do it" was a great agitation in my life. However, like an annoying fly, the Holy Spirit was always in my ear with that love stuff. Love is not puffed up, does not behave rudely, bears all things, believes all things, hopes all things, endures all things...without *complaining*! What?

The presence of anger and disappointment was controlling my mind. Laziness was not tolerated in my life and the *always doing things later plan* digs holes that you sometimes can't get out of. For years, I complained to God about my husband, and I complained to my husband. God's declaration of not taking sides seemed so unfair to me. The instead of *complaining*, do it yourself guide that the Spirit of God was directing me to follow, brought no relief, just added burden. Why should I pick up a grown man's socks? Why do I have to patch the holes in our budget when he swipes "the card" without considering what the money is accounted for? Why do you require more from me because I choose to grow spiritually? Is this a penalty for wanting to be more like You? Then my eyes were opened to these scriptures.

A nagging spouse is like the drip, drip, drip of a leaky faucet; You can't turn it off, and you can't get away from it. Proverbs 27:15 (MSG)

It is better to dwell in a corner of the housetop [on the flat oriental roof, exposed to all kinds of weather] than in a house shared with a nagging, quarrelsome, and faultfinding woman. Proverbs 21:9 (AMP)

    Great conviction came upon me and my heart actually began to hurt for my husband. I felt ashamed that I had put him through so much finger pointing for all those years. But...how do I change when some of my concerns go deeper than a pair of socks. "Dear God, I accept my need to stop nagging but what about him?" I honestly prayed.

    I would be lying if I didn't admit that often I contemplated leaving. I love him, but I wanted peace, at least a plan for peace. One truth kept my feet planted under the same roof with my husband, and it was because I couldn't imagine spending one day of my life without him. The battle in my mind was serious and I knew I was in desperate need of change, immediately!

Shortly after our 24th anniversary, I began to whine (to God) about my husband's need to buy an Icee and a bag of Lay's potato chips everyday. This drove me insane because he never consumed even half of its contents. Me with my systematic planning felt this was such a waste. As I waited for him to complete his purchase, as with violins playing, I began to sing the same song I had sung for all those years to God about this habit not making any sense. I had reached my limit and felt God should have reached His also. As I lifted my eyes and looked at him at the counter, something changed. I didn't see a forty-ish year old man standing there, I saw a child. Painfully, I saw the wound in that child's heart of being told "not today" as he asked for an *Icee* again. That denial, however simple it may seem, created a wound in my husband's heart. As I cried, I realized that God had allowed me to see through His eyes. Yes, God saw waste, but He looked passed that misuse to see a man who vowed he would never be denied to buy what he wanted again, and had compassion. My heart broke for that little boy that was denied long ago. My husband's purchase of such a small product daily was his demonstration of his ability to do so. The product was never consumed because it wasn't his flesh that needed feeding, it was that wounded heart that needed to be silenced. Hurriedly, before he returned, I whispered, "God, help me to wait patiently while he learns that You are not saying *no*."

How Long

Being blessed with this new found compassion helped me to use the grace of God to wipe out complaining about things I didn't like...for a while. Aside from my withdrawal from complaining, I still expected to see evidence that God was working on him also.

Love remains kind even when your mate lives life outside the classroom as if he's never been invited

After having performed my nightly rituals of securing the house, I prepared myself for bed. While turning off the light, I noticed the alarm had been disarmed. Certain that the alarm was set, I asked my husband why it was off. He replied, "I went outside to my truck." My observance of him not resetting the alarm was met with a simple solution of, "just set it again," he said. Simple as that, I thought. Then why didn't he do it? Now here comes an onslaught of my whining about how when he leaves things undone he's not mindful that someone has to do them, and that someone, is always me. "Stop complaining," he commanded, as he playfully kick me in the butt. Resentful that my complaining was being played down, I retaliated with a playful punch to the arm to at least get my lick back while accepting that the real issue would not get resolved.

It was during the wee hours of the morning, after I fulfilled my parental duty of sending my youngest daughter off to another adventure, when I heard, "What if he never changes?" the voice whispered. Tears flowed from my eyes as I sat there speechless evaluating the idea of him never having a plan of order, never considering another way of life. Hours passed before I responded because I knew that it was I who was back in the classroom. Knowing I would never object to being obedient, I guess I just needed to hang onto my right to feel disheartened and that it was me who would submit to the Word once again.

Do all that you can to live in peace with everyone Romans 12:18 (NLT)

"Would you allow love to stop being kind if he never changed?" The Spirit of God continued. I pondered how my requests were rational; redo what you undo, house shoes in the bedroom closet, check bank balance before spending. Nevertheless, I did not put that on my list of needs in a husband, so how could I judge God's request unfair.

The servant who knows what his master wants and ignores it, or insolently does whatever he pleases, will be thoroughly thrashed. But if he does a poor job through ignorance, he'll get off with a slap on the hand. Great gifts mean great responsibilities; greater gifts, greater responsibilities! Luke 12:47-48 (NLT)

The revelation was that God couldn't take sides because neither way was wrong. He used the analogy of me liking oranges and my husband liking apples. I wanted him to like oranges because I do but since that's not his choice, he continues to choose apples. I wanted a spotless home and he was okay with some disorder. Neither way was sin, neither way kept you out of heaven, neither way was eternal. I was asking Him to reprimand my husband about something that was not sin and God was not getting involved in that way. Not disregarding my feelings, God asked me to take the high road and fix whatever needed fixing to me without complaining. No one promised life was fair. The serious matters such as money, He asked me to handle with kindness and to trust Him. "He always made a way," he reminded me. The question of how long rolled to the tip of my tongue before I dismissed it. I learned that love was kind but I also learned that it was not my business how God dealt with the spirit of my husband. I would have to prayerfully remain patient as I suffered, even if it meant that it was long, longer than I would have liked.

From that day forward, I vowed to apply the same rule to my husband as I did my father, just for different reasons. For the sake of peace, when something was out of place, I would correct the situation, but this time with joy. I would not expect my husband to do things the way I did them, I would never expect him to understand my ways. I declared that I would not sweat the stuff that doesn't apply to eternity.

I have sat at the feet of my Teacher and gained great wisdom and I will continue to go back for more since my hunger and thirst for righteousness far outweighs my need to be right. Even though embracing the ways of God are not always easy, I find that His way of doing things do bring great relief. Only God can say to you that you are not wrong in the way you feel or think on one hand, but ask you to sacrifice for the sake of another on the other hand, and you feel at peace. Having greater gifts means having greater responsibilities is not an easy thing to accept, but in order to live Christ-like, enduring these light afflictions are necessary, if love is to be kind.

IT AIN'T EASY, BUT IT'S NECESSARY
Chapter Ten
Old Wounds

Thief

*The thief comes to steal, kill, and destroy...*John 10:10

Walking along a familiar path may spark memories of your first sighting of a deer and her fawn grazing in the grass on a sunny spring day, or maybe an old friend's name coming to mind draws a smile as moments shared causes you to reminisce on the silly times spent together as children growing up. Or maybe like me, the Deceiver, stole your momma's heart toward you, and whenever she saw you, you reminded her of a sad time she had rather not gone through. It's not your fault, nor hers, but somewhere the Deceiver got in and stole your funny baby stories, your cute baby pictures. I don't have any pictures of me as a baby, I don't have any stories of me that don't include a disaster. Me, being burned with hot coffee at eight months old, or me falling on a heater. No one has ever told me one single thing about my growing up as an infant that made them smile or laugh, and I'm convinced that my mother didn't realize the devil stole my beginnings and her love toward me. Life has persuaded me that she doesn't understand that her eyes don't glisten when she sees me, or how much that hurts.

Life is funny. Sometimes there's good and bad things buried beneath the surface, and when found, whether it's gold or dynamite, the explosion changes your life forever.

Last Straw

When God does housecleaning, no sin, no secret, is left hidden.

I was thirty-five years old when all the resentment toward my mother came boiling to the top and shattered my peace. No one knew the monstrosity that had laid smoldering within me as I walked through life smiling. I didn't know! Hearing about yet another eventful time spent with my brother, my brother, my brother...was more than I could bear. I exploded!

All the memories of being second, being nothing, being forgettable took over my heart. The things that crushed me I am sure she didn't remember. She would probably be shocked to know they mattered to me because I never protested against her actions. I just accepted my place in my family.

"Mom, did you realize that when I was visiting with you at your home and the doorbell rang, that you never came back into the room where I was. I waited assuming you and your guest would come and join me. I waited. Soon I realized that you had forgotten I was even there, so I left. You never called to apologize for your oversight. You never told my brother that I was even in the house."

"Do you realize your eye twinkled when you looked at my brother and even now they twinkle when you look at his son and grandson."

"I want them to twinkle for me! I don't want to just be your daughter by blood, I want to be your daughter by heart. M o m m a, can you hear me? "

"You are my strong child!" were the words my mother would say. If I had a quarter for every time I was told that, I would be a wealthy woman. People use pacifiers to help quieten the echoes of their hearts. I believe my mother felt my strength gave her a pardon to unintentionally ignore my existence.

Being strong was not a dishonor, but in my family, as a girl child, it was a curse. I didn't mind being able to stand on my own, but when I was a child, a young girl, I needed a watchful eye to steer me through the ever changing paths of my life.

There was a continual pattern throughout my life. When it came to the matters of the heart I was forgettable, but whenever there was a difficult situation, I was always the problem solver, the fixer, the shoulder to be leaned on. There was always a fire in someone's life that needed extinguishing; my mother, my brother, his wife, his children, his grandchildren. When my brother got on his feet, his children took his place in my mother's life. After them their children. I'm not blaming any of them though, my brother's children were victims of two parents that were swallowed up by the world of darkness. Regrettably, the domino effect cast them into the same pit I was subject to, the absentee father, the absentee mother, and no real place to land.

Despite it all, I clawed my way through life, with no self-help manual, trying to figure out which way was up. I was strong because something within me wouldn't give up and die. Knowing, but not understanding, that there was a force constantly with me. *"For You formed my inward parts; You covered me in my mother's womb."* Psalm 139:13 Great was God's mercy and grace toward me.

When I was fifty-three years old, my mom apologized to me for having neglected me. I was dumbfounded, speechless. My mind wanted to run down the list of all the ways she had neglected me, abandoned me, forgotten me, but...the fight in my heart was depleted and I had long given up on ever being recognized. I was speechless, I simply cried.

God's Gift

That apology was coordinated by God. It came at a time in our life when we had suffered a tremendous loss. God knew I needed my mom and she needed me, too. Not to fix anything, just to help each other walk through this dark valley.

God helped me dissolve my anger toward my mother by bluntly telling me "to get over it and stop dwelling on what she didn't do and dwell on what she did: gave me life. *She did her best."*

"Anyone who intends to come with Me has to let Me lead. You're not in the driver's seat—I am. Don't run from suffering; embrace it. Follow Me and I'll show you how. Self-help is no help at all. Self-sacrifice is the way, My way, to finding yourself, your true self. What good would it do to get everything you want and lose you, the real you? Luke 9:23-25 MSG

My mom's mother was a strong and persuasive woman. Her control existed over only one person like that, my mother. The irony was that my grandmother was my mother's dependent. When my grandfather died my mom, only fifteen, became the head of her family. My grandmother pulled her load, but never outside the presence of my mom. Until the day she died at the age of eighty-nine, my grandmother influenced my mom's every move. That must have been a lot of pressure to live under. My grandmother was a "taking care of business" type person. She took care of the home while my mom worked, but she ran our home like a business. She made sure that you were well fed, but she never hugged you. You had the freshest clothes and the cleanest and safest home, but she never said she loved you. From all the lessons she learned in life, she gave you her all. Unfortunately, nothing had anything to do with the act of love, just the act of responsibility. Out of her womb, she birthed my mother and instilled in her the same work ethic. They were the Martha's, always working but never sitting down to enjoy the fruits of their labor and never sitting down to enjoy love.

"She did her best!" "God, whose life were you watching?" I asked. "She did her best," He whispered. No matter how close I was to God, He would not alter His stand to pacify the licking of my wounds. He is kind and compassionate to us all, and He really does look beyond our faults and sees our hearts. I know that my mother never intentionally hurt me, but she did. Her mother never intentionally hurt her either, but she did. Nevertheless, God's Word, I am taught in Hebrews 4:12, *is powerful and a discerner of the thoughts and intents of the heart.* Therefore, I believed God. She did her best!

Even though my mom was never a touchy-feely type person, she worked her butt off to provide for me and my brother and never asked my dad for a dime. My mother is a strong, proud woman, who still doesn't reveal her pains often, but in her own way, she cares. There's no mountain in the world my mother wouldn't move for me if she could. She did love me, I know now, as best she knew how.

We hand down to each generation the things we've learned whether good or bad. My mother was handed what her mother knew and I was handed what my mother knew. The one thing the devil couldn't control was my breakthrough with God. In that new found freedom that evaded my family for decades, I learned to love the unlovable. I learned to give respect regardless of whether it was returned. I learned to honor God in all I did and look to Him to repay me, and repay, He does. It wasn't easy, but for the sake of peace and my continuous blessings in God, it was most definitely necessary that I learn to forgive.

IT AIN'T EASY, BUT IT'S NECESSARY
Chapter Eleven
Through the Valley of Death

Yea, though I walk through the valley of the shadow of death, I will fear no evil. Psalm 23

When living a surrendered life in submission to the Spirit of God, you live as if you're standing on a cliff with your hands in the air, following His lead. It's blind trust. Can God deceive me? There's no evil in God, so I'll say no, He can't deceive me and my uplifted hands symbolize that I don't believe He ever would.

My life took an unexpected turn in August of 2009. My only sibling began a walk through the valley of death, and there was nothing I could do about it.

For twenty-seven years, my brother lived a life with a drug and alcohol addiction. Anyone who has been remotely acquainted with an addict knows that their problems spill over into the lives of everyone close to them. His dependency on drugs affected the lives of his wife, his children, his mother, and me, his sister.

In respect to my brother, I would like to clarify, that before his death, he wrote his story and gave me permission to use it for the good of others.

My knowledge of his journey with drugs began in 1973, the year we graduated from high school. My mother had made the discovery of his usage and they were talking supposedly outside of my hearing range. I tuned the conversation out as it became repetitive until his comment caught my attention when he said, "I'm not hurting anyone but myself." At that moment, in my mind, I sided with him, he wasn't hurting me, I shrugged. But years of watching his body deteriorate, watching him abuse his finances, (he was a functioning addict), and watching him neglect his wife and kids, pushed my vote against him in the end. You were hurting someone other than yourself, you were even hurting me.

Looking back now, I can see how the Spirit of God coordinated the developments of my life all the way up to his death. In 1999, after numerous rounds in rehabilitation centers, my brother began his journey of being drug free after 27 years of abuse. He was free from alcohol, drugs, and cigarettes, when suddenly, in 2005, he suffered an attack of acute abdominal pains which eventually led to a trip to the emergency room. After a number of test, doctors discovered that my brother had metastatic liver cancer. It's frightening to receive a telephone call that informs you that your loved one is hospitalized and the diagnosis is grave. The walk into his hospital room brought my courage face to face with his. I wanted to be anything but brave. I wanted to throw myself across the foot of his bed and cry out to God, "Why me, God? This is *my* only sibling; what will I do without him; how can *I* bear to see him suffer; why God, why?" It sounds so dramatic and selfish, but we process everything according to the way it affects us before we come to our senses and realize that *he* is the one truly suffering. Sparing him all my theatrical performances, I approached him with my spiritual face in order to comfort my brother and hear the game plan. Now comes his face, filled with courage while asking me if I'm okay. Me, knowing what he really wanted to say is, Sis, I'm scared out of my mind. What in the world is going on with me? Why? Courage spoke back, "don't worry about me, you're the one I'm concerned about, you're the one going through." After a lot of blabbing, speaking but not saying anything, hearing but not listening, I knelt by his bed, took his hand, and prayed. "Dear God, it is because of Jesus we can come boldly to petition You for Your help. You are the only answer that matters, You are the only One that's all knowing..." After closing the prayer, a man in a white coat said *amen* as he rose from his knees right beside me. The Christian surgeon.

As stated in Jeremiah 29:11, God had a plan for good and not evil because it was against all medical advice to operate on Arthur's liver. Doctors believed the cancer had advanced to a stage where it was beyond their abilities. Miraculously, the same Christian doctor that bowed in prayer combined his faith with Arthur's faith to perform the surgery. I believe God purposely hid the size of the tumor from the doctors, because even the Christian doctor would have withdrawn if he had known that the tumor housed more than two-thirds of his liver. Once inside there was no turning back and upon completion, my brother was left with one-third of a sick liver, the outlook was grim. They sent him to the intensive care recovery room to die. One hour stretched into another and still he was alive. No heroic measures were ever necessary as his vital signs were normal and his health continually improved. Much to the surprise of the medical staff, Arthur lived throughout the night and was moved to a regular room the next day. Within five days he was released from the hospital, but before he departed, his doctor paraded him in front of all the other liver patients to show them how faith works beyond doctors' knowledge. Against all odds, my brother became the first person in Shreveport's history to survive liver cancer.

Wanting a second opinion, once strong enough, Arthur was sent to M. D. Anderson Hospital, in Houston, Texas. His doctor wanted the experts to consult with them on Arthur's future treatment. Despite the miraculous surgery, the Anderson doctors did not believe my brother's liver would ever be strong enough for him to live a healthy life. But God had other plans. Before returning home Arthur stopped for a bite to eat. While waiting for his food, a police officer stopped by his table and asked if he could pray with him. Such a strange request coming from someone who was a complete stranger. Needing all the prayers he could get, my brother gladly joined hands with the officer and received his blessings. It turned out that the officer was a member of Joel Osteen's church and he felt led to say that though the reports were gloomy, trust God. Arthur was amazed that God had sent him a *ray of hope*. This man didn't know him or his condition, yet he was courageous enough to stand in the middle of a restaurant and pray. True to His word, my brother was a living witness to the goodness of God in the land of the living. His liver did get stronger and grew back healthy, and Arthur lived a productive life.

Business as Usual

God had mercifully spared Arthur's life from several circumstances he faced while living a life in the darkness of drugs. I assumed that after having been spared from death once again by the mercy of God, this was the time when Arthur would rise up to do the work God had called him to do. He had faithfully attended Louisiana Baptist Bible College, where he obtained a degree in Theology. He loved to study the Word of God, and was faithful in his attendance of church. It was however, his inability to untangle his life with the mothers of his children that got in the way of his relationship with God. His choices infuriated me as I could not understand how someone could have experienced such a divine touch from God and still not make Jesus the number one priority in his life. He was trying and I realized that, but his trust was in his efforts to figure things out, and it just wasn't working. He would forever be the father of his children, but it was time he crowned someone the Mrs. and set the others free.

He had such a kind heart that he just couldn't hurt anyone, so he hurt himself.

I was angry at my brother, angry at his decisions, but...inwardly, I had a knowing that time was running out. I was resentful that he had spent so many years creating complicated dilemmas in his life that were derived from fleshly pleasures. The women were big girls and they should have protected themselves but the children were innocent and they deserved his best. I was angry for me also. I worked with my brother, lived in the same neighborhood as he did, but still never had an opportunity to spend any quality time with him. It was just the two of us, no one else could share our memories of listening to the radio while sitting at the kitchen table or sitting up in the big oak tree in the back yard for hours during the summer months, just talking. I missed my brother. I had lost so many years when he was involved with drugs and now I just wanted some part of his life that was special, rather than passing in the wind.

During a time in 2009 when Spring was beginning to come in, life as I knew it began to fall apart. My mother grew ill and had to have emergency surgery. This and other events hurled her into depression. In the course of caring for her, I understood clearly what God meant when

He gave to us because of His love, not because of our actions. She was difficult to care for because she was depressed but God supplied the grace needed to look past her mean spiritedness and understand her pain. My brother and I were able to nurse her back to health. After two surgeries, she was finally back on her feet and caring for herself by July and my relationship with Arthur was strengthened. I stopped looking at what he was doing wrong and focused on how much more God loved him than I ever could. This brought a peace between us and we continued to talk and text just to say *love you* surpassing a surmountable hurdle. God had set the stage.

On August 11th, the sound of my mother's voice told me that something was wrong. As I hurried to the hospital I prayed, "Lord help my family, we're under attack!" Upon arriving, I learned my brother needed surgery because there was bleeding on his brain. My mother had just become independent of needing our help and now this! God whispered to my spirit, "Mary, you have to fight for your family." One week later, after praying with him, I watched Arthur go into surgery. Once more, God's glory beamed forth. After removing a portion of my brother's skull, the tumor and fluid flowed out without the surgeon ever putting a scalpel on his brain.

The doctor was amazed and thankful that they did not have to do any invasive procedures. Arthur was fine and was given a positive prognosis. Four days later, he was released from the hospital.

In the meantime, thirteen days later, on August 31st, my oldest daughter had a life changing surgery. The battle was on, but I knew it was not bigger than my God. I was not losing my family to this enemy. My spirit, soul, and body were tired but quitting was not an option.

As a Christian committed to seeking God and His way of doing things, our growth at times comes without clarity. God's way does not always appear right and my limited knowledge, my limited understanding does not always bring comfort even though I know God is on my side. Circumstances sometimes clouds my seeing Him or His love in those moments. My mind questions how a God that says He loves me can allow these struggles to come. If God is as sovereign as I have learned Him to be, then why not do it in a way my mind and my heart can understand. Why are His acts in puzzle like form? I was wrestling and I knew by then that God knew what was on my heart so I had learned to come respectfully and bring honesty to the table. "Why not just lay the map, the plan out on the table," I reason. "God…I don't want a piece here and a piece there. I don't want to leave shaking my head wandering what just happened. I just want to sit in conference with you like Abraham did when he discussed the pending fallout of Sodom. That's the way we've worked before, but now, my Father, You have changed Your strategy on me. I feel as if You have called a forum to discuss the fate of my family but for some reason, this time my name is not on the list of attendees."

Dear Heavenly Father, guide my footsteps as I walk this path in a bewildered state.

After testing proved that the mass removed from Arthur's brain was cancerous, my job was to keep my brother's spirit encouraged, but that was difficult as he faced one bad report after another one. I couldn't let those reports shake me though, I had to rely on God's love, I had to trust Him. At that Point, my biggest fight was a war against me losing hope.

September 20th

While traveling to minister at Elayn Hunt Correctional Center in Baton Rouge, Louisiana, once again my phone rang. I ordered my niece to call 911 as it appeared my brother was having a stroke. "Lord, what's happening? I can't see, it's dark, but I trust You because I know there is no one greater to turn to. Help!"

Two days later, I put the celebration of my anniversary on hold as everything changed when I was summoned once again to immediately return to the hospital. After a battery of tests, the last one scheduled, an echogram, revealed that Arthur had another clot in the left ventricle of his heart that was breaking into pieces and traveling to his brain producing stroke like symptoms. The nurse came in and administered an injection to help thin my brother's blood in hopes of slowing down the inevitable. The laughter, the smiles that filled the room less than two hours ago were gone as she stated with certainty that the clot would definitely take his life at any given moment. There were no ifs, ands, or buts, just a clear cut announcement that my brother, my only sibling, would die without notice.

I later learned that this type of clot was often found in habitual drug abusers. Even though, he had been drug free for ten years, the abuse was taking its toll on his body. I looked into my brother's face as a tear rolled from his eye. My assignment was to stand in the face of this devastating news and keep him hopeful. I placed my headphones on his ears as I piped in inspirational songs reminding him of God and His greatness. I needed to buy myself time. I needed a corner to shrink into as I fought to keep hope within myself as I walked through this valley of death with my brother.

I quoted every healing scripture I knew. I declared and decreed every confession that called death a lie and God miraculous. I reiterated my trust and dependency on my Heavenly Father. I gripped doubt by the neck as I fought against the knowledge of man in order to declare God all knowing. Despite all I knew to do, I needed to hear the Spirit of God's plan, I needed to be included in the conference between the Deity. "What's happening, Daddy? What are You doing?" I sensed Him instructing, "Trust! Look not to your own weaknesses or inabilities. I will guide you."

Thinking back, I had always prayed for my brother's deliverance, but in 2005, I took on the battle for the life of my brother's soul because I didn't want him to go to hell. There was a sense of doom lurking. I felt something was on the horizon for him and it did not feel good. Arthur had run in his own strength but I discerned that time was running out. He ran his life according to his wisdom, devising a plan that deceived others as well as himself. The traps of life had caused him to stretch himself in ways not approved by God. Unintentionally, he was doing everything in his power to inch as close to destruction as he could come without going over and even that was by the mercy of God. Arthur was trying to fix his life without hurting others and that was impossible. When Light shines on truth, lies are revealed, which brings pain before deliverance. There's no way around it, but Arthur was trying to avoid that road.

    Drugs and alcohol can take a family to places that aren't meant for the weak at heart. I have never indulged in the activity of putting illegal drugs in my body, but I have witnessed the devastating disruption they cause and the ruins they leave behind. As I stood in the intensive care unit where they abruptly moved my brother, I learned that the 27 years of abuse had once again reared its ugly head. As I held the power of attorney over his affairs, I perceived all the mayhem that was going on had nothing to do with the seen. "Dad, what are You doing? I prayed." I looked at the brave face Arthur was putting on in the face of a faithful companion, but I knew he heard the same thing I heard. I knew he had to be scared. Thank goodness, they medicated him to make him rest, I needed the break to pray for directions.

The nurse, after confirming my authority to make decisions on his behalf, approached me and asked me to sign a do not resuscitate order. She advised that if they tried to revive him the compression on his chest would only push the floating clots further into his heart which would result in instant death anyway. She said the situation was hopeless and because of her certainty, she allowed us to move chairs into the intensive care room, to await that irrefutable moment she expected that night. "Do not sign it," the Lord instructed! The look on the nurses's face informed me that my lack of education was no match for her knowledge and her on the job experience. Feeling no need to reveal my inside source, I trusted my inward witness and stood my ground.

One day turned into another as the nurses changed shifts only to return and find Arthur still alive. Their efforts to keep Arthur still were growing more futile as he grew weary of being so long in bed. They couldn't explain why he was still among the land of the living, but I could. God was doing something that was not transparent, but in my heart, I knew He was bringing a plan into fruition.

From the looks of things, it troubled me that Arthur might not be taking his prognosis seriously. If faced with indisputable death, I feel my last possible days would be spent getting all my affairs in order. I would be sitting before God in such an obvious way that others would feel a need to bow before His throne upon entering my room. Knowing my brother like I did, his mouth was not revealing what his mind was thinking. He needed time to spend alone instead of keeping his reputation up in the presence of others. Others, that didn't recognize that something was happening in the unseen that would soon change all our worlds. Even those that had accepted that he would possibly die were not aware of the seriousness of what takes place at death. The crossing into eternity, be it with God or without God, is the most pertinent decision that must be made before the last breath is drawn. Quietly I prayed, "Daddy, please don't let my brother go to hell."

This had become a prayer I often prayed for Arthur throughout the last four years of his life. I had petitioned heaven. I had made declarations until I was depleted. Exhausted, one day I grew weary. The Spirit of God sensing my fatigue, encouraged me not to give up. So in faith, I shortened my prayers to pray for what the bottom line is for us all, not to spend eternity in hell.

Witnessing the "I" syndrome playing out in Arthur's life only exposed that he had worn himself out trying to appease everyone. He was seeking positions to validate himself in the lives of too many, but God wasn't allowing it. In one breath, he promised one mother of his child the world and turned and submitted that same promise to another mother of another child. While yet, another mother of a third child stood in the wings understanding he had gotten himself into a mess that only the truth could dissolve. To her, he promised to tell the truth so that he could live his life in peace. He sought approval from the hearts of women more broken than he was. Two, three, four broken messes trying to emerge as one. *I heard the Lord laugh.*

Peace evaded my brother's life as he lived under the same curse as our father, the desire to enjoy the fruit of all the women they met, not realizing that too much fruit only causes diarrhea. Our father died unhappily tangled in a web at the mercy of a woman he had betrayed others with. Then he betrayed her. When he became weak from the effects that cancer caused his body, she executed her revenge. Her care for him was mostly sublet to her mother and upon his death she buried him in a double knitted chocolate brown suit with beige stitching, while giving his finer updated suits to her son. During the viewing of his body, I shook my head as the disgraceful display she presented of my dad proved that an angry woman is a force to be reckoned with.

September 26

Four days after being put on watch, Arthur experienced another breaking off of the clot that brought on stroke like symptoms again but this time it caused him to ease into a comatose state. My brother's daughter called, "Aunt Mary, Daddy had another episode, they said you better come quickly." Running and praying at the same time, I requested, "Daddy, I don't know what you're doing, but today is my mother's birthday, don't let him die today, please."

After taking him for x-rays, we were later informed that the brain had started to swell and there were also small cancerous spots on his lungs that were very treatable, if he could beat this clot. Miraculously, he didn't die and later in the evening, once again to the amazement of the nurses, he awakened to life again. I made a suggestion to the cardiologist that since they didn't have a tool to remove the clot without it dissolving and causing damage to the heart or brain, to put him on the transplant list. She was excited of that possibility and was assured with his pending doom, he would go to the top of the list. "Thank you Lord!" I shouted. The excitement was short lived though as the cardiologist called the next day disappointed that Arthur couldn't be added to the transplant list until he had been cancer free for one year. Having just had the brain hemorrhaging procedure last month put him a long way off from making a year. "What now, Daddy?"

    Physically drained, I persuaded my niece that she and I were taking the next day off and letting her brother sit with Arthur while we got some much needed rest. My brother spent some quality time with his son that day in between resting. However, once again, toward nightfall, the phone rung, this time it took me by surprise. It was my brother!

"Sis, I need to tell you something. God made you a fighter and I know you are tired but don't stop, because people like me need you. I have been in a lot of dark places when I sleep and I hear voices; but the one voice I hear above all, is yours. And when I hear your voice, you lead me to the Light. I know you are tired, but don't stop fighting, Sis. God gave you that gift." I said,

"Brother, hurry and get well, so that you can help me in this fight." He said, *"I'll always be with you, Sis, I'll always be with you."*

God used my brother to speak His plan to me. In volumes, God spoke that Arthur was not going to get well on this side but that he was headed to the light. He also said, that this assignment for my life was exhausting but much needed. People, like me, need you. "People like who, God?" I asked. People who were not spiritually strong enough to fight the spirits of darkness to get home, he impressed upon my heart. I cried! My only sibling had just told me he was leaving, there is no other way he could always be with me. He also told me he needed me to get him to eternity with God, to which I had not realized the depth.

As I had to continue to go to work, my beautifully faithful niece stood watch with her dad. "Aunt Mary, Daddy keeps jerking. They say he's having seizures." "I'll be there after work," I replied. I went into my prayer closet where the Spirit of God revealed to me that my brother was being tormented by the spirits of darkness. He was not having seizures, they were trying to convince him to give up getting to the Light. "You must fight, Mary," the Spirit of God impressed.

"Lord, have mercy on my son...He has seizures and is suffering greatly...Jesus replies, ..."Bring the boy here to me." Jesus rebuked the demon, and it came out of the boy, and he was healed from that moment. Matthew 17:15-18) NKJ

When I walked into Arthur's room, I asked my niece to leave me alone with him. Through my studies, I knew that even though my brother's body was comatose, his spirit man was alive and functioning. I got into his physical ear and spoke to his spiritual ear. "You tormenting spirits of darkness, LEAVE MY BROTHER ALONE, NOW! YOU WILL NOT PREVENT HIM FROM REACHING THE LIGHT!" To God's glory, Arthur never jerked again. He slept peacefully! Armed with wisdom, I was ready to do whatever God willed for me.

I was approached again about the DNR, this time by my mother and the nurse. I understood their reasoning for wanting me to sign the DNR but I also knew that it was not in my hands but in the Hands of God to do whatever, whenever. Arthur had not only given me power of attorney over decisions but he had made me executor of his will. He wanted to spare his adult children and his mother the burden of what such decisions could bring. I did not know that when he asked me to perform such tasks, if needed, that God was orchestrating my brother's life and keeping His promise to me to not let him go to hell. If a person that was not sensitive to the voice of God was in charge of these decisions, they could rely on medical advice only and interfere with God's divine timing.

    I explained to my mother and the nurse that I was waiting on the Spirit of God to guide me each step. I told them that they were concerned with my brother's physical health only, but I was mainly concerned with his spirit man. I agreed with them that resuscitating him would not help. However, I also knew that the only time you resuscitate is when someone is dead, so if resuscitating would kill him, he can't get any deader, so why stress? By now I had become angry; She was a nurse that was coaching my mother to agree with her. In all those days, not one doctor had come by, even though they were getting paid for ordering tests. I informed her that every doctor that was getting a dime from my brother's insurance needed to come and talk with me personally or I would inform the insurance company of the fraud. It's astonishing how money affects people. Within the next two hours, four doctors came by. Two of which, I didn't even know were aware of his case. As God continued to arrange my brother's steps, one doctor gave me information that God intended for me to know. When it was time to move, I would understand when God said now.

The same nurse pushing the DNR was the same one that had allowed us to stay in the ICU. She was kicking herself because seven days later Arthur was still holding on and she resented my stand. I now know that the allowed chairs was a plan God had for me to keep access to Arthur. God was guarding my brother's spirit. He had placed watch over words of destruction invading his life. It was time for quietness, time for God to work. Hallelujah!

As my niece sat with him, she would trust my instructions to guard him. My husband came in to stand guard with him on Tuesday night for me. He called me that next morning to say that my brother had a bad rattling in his chest as he breathed. The doctor that God used had told me that would be the death rattle and time was drawing near. I didn't get alarmed, I just kept listening to God. After work Wednesday, I came and sat with my brother. I knew my time for leaving him was over. God had even advised me that it was time to sign the DNR order. It had been days since he was awake and I had done all that I was humanly capable of doing, so I whispered to him, "Brother, I've done all I can do, it's up to you now. It's between you and God. Pray!" He never opened his eyes, but as assuredly as God is our god, Arthur said to me audibly, "I'm praying Sis!"

His body had failed him, but his spirit was fighting on to reach that Light! There is no quit in the part of us that lives forever. I had become acquainted with the power of our spiritual bodies but this reinforced that we are simply housed in a body where a soul and spirit dwells and never dies.

Getting a quick relief, I went home to stay with my daughter until my husband returned from out of town. After showering, as I waited, I drifted off. My husband awoke me and insisted that I sleep a little longer before going back to the hospital. "I couldn't,' I informed him, 'I have to get back." I went into the bedroom with the full intentions of getting dressed and leaving but my weary body convinced me that I could lay down for just a hour. As quickly as my head hit my pillow, a vision of my brother came to me. He was dressed in slacks, a sweater, and he had a hat on his head cocked to the side in a sassy way. It was so like my brother, to look cool. He tilted his head to the side and looked at me with his hands in his pockets while standing on the side of a hill. Instantly, I jumped up saying, "I'm coming. You're waiting on me, I'm coming!"

Hurriedly, but without any fear or hesitation, I entered his room. My relief was sitting with him and upon my entering we exchanged looks. I went to his bedside to let him know I was back. I told him that I saw him dressed and standing on the side of a hill. "You're ready to go over to the other side, aren't you?" I said, not really asking. "Okay, I want you to know that I will take care of mom and your children. I'll watch over them, I give you my word." I requested that the nurse come in and suction him and give him something for pain. Information from *the doctor* also gave me knowledge that he would be in pain and the morphine toward the end would slow his heart down. Knowing what I was asking, the nurse said, "Are you sure," to which I replied, "yes." I had gotten the word from God, it was time, His time. As the medicine took its affect and his blood pressure and heart began to slow, I walked over to him for the last time and said, "I have walked as far as I possibly can, it's time for you to make that big giant step toward the *Light* now, but alone.

Whenever you're ready, go toward the light to Jesus. I'll see you one day on the other side. Cheer for me, okay!"

On October 1st of 2009, at 3:45 a.m., my brother, at the age of 54, began his journey with Jesus. I cried, but I praised God that my brother did not go to hell.

He's Gone

The next things that followed proved to be a whirlwind of events that needed to be taken care of. The phones calls were the hardest: "Mom, he's gone," was my first, and from there the tears continued with each number I dialed. My brother, her son, their dad...was gone!

I was totally taken by surprised when my mom asked me to do my brother's funeral services. I had not heard anything like that from the Spirit of God, so I told her that I would pray about it, but I didn't think so. So much like God, He informed me that it was time to begin telling my brother's story at his services. "You will have an audience there that you will never see again," God implied.

But because God was so gracious, so very generous, here I am. And I'm not about to let his grace go to waste. Haven't I worked hard trying to do more than any of the others? Even then, my work didn't amount to all that much. It was God giving me the work to do, God giving me the energy to do it. So whether you heard it from me or from those others, it's all the same: We spoke God's truth and you entrusted your lives. I Corinthians 15:10-11 (MSG)

I knew doing the eulogy at Arthur's services was allowing God to reach inside of me and it was one of the hardest things I had ever done. By God's grace, the six souls that dedicated their lives were worth the efforts. At the gravesite, I hugged and spoke to several of the guys that ran with Arthur. They acknowledged that it was only by God's hand that they were still alive. They understood the gift they had been given. They too, had reached out to Jesus while there was still breath. They thanked me for telling my brother's story. It opened their eyes to God's goodness.

It's not easy being a woman in a male dominated calling. I surely felt the many daggers aimed at me when I walked up in that pulpit. I didn't walk into the pulpit of the *God didn't call no women preachers pulpit*, I walked onto the platform of the funeral home's pulpit. I didn't ask permission, I simply followed God's leading. It wasn't easy, but without a doubt the Spirit of God had my back, and my mission would not be deterred because of man's rules that have nothing to do with salvation. It was necessary that the plan of God be executed as I began my journey for people, who like my brother, needed me to fight for them.

IT AIN'T EASY, BUT IT'S NECESSARY
Chapter Twelve
Too Soon

After having completed the task of laying my brother, my only sibling, to rest, I had some quiet time. Unexpectedly, two weeks afterward it hit me, my brother was gone; dead. Wow! The waterfall came, the agony hit with a vengeance. My brother died. "God, why? It was too soon and I fully expected him to recover. Why?"

Arthur had beat the odds so many times. God had been so merciful to him. He had protected him from the seen and I know the unseen. The parts that I knew of were mind blowing. I told God, I never wanted to know the unknown. Still, he had survived a fight with two brothers who were secretly armed with knives. When it ended, he had ten stab wounds. One right above the heart, one an inch below his eye, and another to the side that had punctured his lung. Even though the street was full of people, no one raised a hand to help. *When you use and deal drugs real friends are few*, as quoted by Arthur.

He told of a dream he had after being rushed to surgery. While unconscious, he dreamt he was standing in the middle of the road and it was very dark. But in the distance he could see a very dim light. He remembered feeling afraid, mostly because he didn't know how to reach the light. He began walking through the incredible darkness and came to a fork in the road where a figure was standing as the road split. Frightened, he began running, trying to get away from the figure, when suddenly it yelled, "STOP, you're going the wrong way." Slowly, he said he started to see the light again but as he began to wake up from the anesthesia, his eyes fell on the faces of his wife and mother. He knew that he was alive because of divine intervention. God had worked a miracle on his behalf.

It was so ironic that the dream was the same as the one Arthur told me about before he died in 2009. The first dream happened in the late 1970s and I didn't discover it until I read his writings after his death.

On another occasion, Arthur was so high and intoxicated that he allowed a young lady, who had never driven a day in her life, to drive my mother's car. While trying to pass another car on a narrow bridge, she drove head on into it. My brother received a cut so severe on his arm that his two small fingers remained drawn up from severe nerve damage that couldn't be repaired.

Nevertheless, he survived. Liver cancer, he survived; brain hemorrhaging from a tumor that was cancerous, he survived. Working in a car factory with massive robots while in an inebriated state every day for years; he survived without ever getting physically hurt. However, there was an embarrassing moment when he had laced a marijuana cigarette with embalming fluid and smoked it on his lunch break. That day was peculiar as I ended up talking him down off a brand new truck's hood. He was sitting there singing *Sitting on the Dock of the Bay by Otis Redding*. There in front of our co-workers, my brother's drug addiction had taken him to a new low, but he survived.

The cost was great though. He experienced the death of his wife as she lost her battle to the drugs he introduced her to, leaving behind three children who were now the sole responsibility of a drugged out daddy. Though, guilt ridden, He survived! He had a very dear friend and co-worker die in his arms from heart failure, others that did time in prison, had heart attacks, one's mind so destroyed that he wandered the streets not knowing who he was or where he was going until his death. One living on dialysis for his kidneys, another waiting on a liver transplant. Numerous others suffering various physical struggles. He had directly and indirectly experienced it all. "So why now, God, why didn't he survive this time?" I wondered.

I made a trip to a cabin where I had found comfort many times when I needed to hear from God. I walked around the land as I waited to hear the Spirit of God's voice. "You taught me to come and let us reason together. But this time, You did not talk with me about the final results. Talk to me, Daddy, please," I begged. "It was his best time," God spoke. "It was his best time to come to Me. If I had consulted with you, would you have let him go," God asked? I took a moment to reflect. I knew it would be fruitless to lie. "No,' I replied, 'it was too soon." Silence followed and I knew His answer was what it was; it was Arthur's best time to make it into heaven. Previous knowledge comforted me as I was grateful that God did what was best for Arthur rather than consider my loss of him. After all, that was my prayer, don't let my brother go to hell.

His leaving was still hard to accept, so one day I stopped by the gravesite, something I didn't practice. There's no one there, just boxes and decayed bodies awaiting their resurrection. That day, however, I needed to be close to Arthur, so I visited his grave. I was not prepared for the grief that consumed me. My mind fought with the idea that his body was underneath that dirt. I wanted to claw down those six feet to retrieve that box. I was not foolish, it was not the box I wanted, it was Arthur. I hurried to my car to hide the flow of tears that I couldn't control. "God, I'm happy my brother is with You, I just miss him so much."

People who don't seek God have no clue how merciful He is. He never scolded me about my sadness, in fact, I felt so consoled by His understanding that it took a minute to adjust to the loss of a loved one. I was not crying without hope, my soul was just hurting. For my sake, during praise and worship one Wednesday night at church, while my arms were lifted toward heaven, I saw a vision of my brother. He got out of his hospital bed, totally healed, still dressed in the hospital gown, and walked straight past me. Startled, I immediately sought answers from within. The Spirit of God explained the vision. "If he would have been healed, he would have gone back to doing things his way, and been lost forever this time. His body would have failed him without any warning and no time for repentance. This was his best time." I was lost for words because I know now that my brother knows better than me that his choices on earth, though well intended, were not God's will.

"People like me need you Sis." People like me need to be snatched from the fires of hell.

My brother's departure from this earth was too soon. He was too young. I believe that if he was 102 and I was 101 and God asked me to let him go, I would have still said, "No, God, it's too soon!" It isn't easy to yield to God's will sometimes, but I have learned for the sake of all involved, it's necessary to let go and just trust God.

IT AIN'T EASY BUT IT'S NECESSARY
Chapter Thirteen
I'll Never Forget

Sometimes when my mind wanders I can easily slip into the *what if* modes. What if I was…can lead down a lot of avenues that realistically are only fantasies that can never be fully realized. I will never be taller but I can create an allusion that I am by wearing a shoe with heels that will allow me to extend my height. I will never have green eyes but I can purchase contacts that will, for a time, allow me to modify my appearance. Truthfully though, when I remove all that I could have purchased to create the me I wish I could be, nothing will be different, just temporarily altered.

I will always be who I am, from where I came, and for whatever reason, why! Some answers lie in the realms of heaven and if God chooses to reveal them to us while here on earth, He will. If He doesn't, then we will have to trust Him and wait until all things that are hidden are revealed.

Our weakness lies in failing to trust. Trusting takes commitment. Commitment that despite what we see on earth, we believe, we trust in God's Word. Commitment that despite what we feel, we trust in God's Way. We have never seen Jesus, but something within us knows that He exists. Many have called us fools, but as I sit here witnessing the greening of the earth after having shed its' winter covering, I know that God keeps His word. For He said in Genesis 8:22, that *"While the earth remains, seedtime and harvest, cold and heat, winter and summer, and day and night shall not cease."* In all the years that I have been privileged to live on this earth, I have yet to witness a time when the seasons did not yield to each other and when day did not turn into night. I am not professing to be such a student of the Bible that I can declare that I know or understand everything about God, because I don't. I have spent many moments resisting the urge to shake my fist toward heaven and ask why. Truthfully, minus the fist shaking, there have been times when I have asked why. Not in a disrespectful way, but in a searching way, like a child seeking knowledge from their parent. I would be lying if I said that I always received the answers I looked for, but I can say that I have always received comfort that God was right there on the scene. Right there, I found a place to rest. A place to lay the burden that plagued me down. No, the wrong didn't disappear, no the unpleasantness wasn't whisked away, but the sting, the heaviness was gone. The presence of God being invited to our situation brings peace, brings rest. Our trust comes from accepting His Way! In the days of the Bible, many turned away from Jesus because He didn't appear to them in the manner that they expected, (John 6:60). They were accustomed to a king that sat on a throne that barked out orders that all obeyed because of fear, not respect. Jesus came preaching faith with words of love, not condemning lightning bolts. He asked people to trust that His words were words of life, eternal life that only the Spirit can give. My almost meditating myself out of my body proved that human efforts are fruitless to permanent solutions, (John 6:63), and only when I executed dependency on God and His teachings did I find a sense of calmness no matter the situation.

    The phrase "Milkman's Baby" brought a lot of pain and unnecessary agony into my life, and yes, had my parents known Jesus and His Way, I could have been spared this reckless episode of events that, at so many times, could have cost me my life. That however, falls into the category of *what if*. I could compare myself with a baby that was aborted or left in an orphanage to estimate that things could have been worse. Be that as it may, isn't evil just evil? Man ranks sin on a scale of bad to worse, but aren't they still all wrongs? Isn't a liar just as wrong as a thief, and in reality aren't they much of the same? Doesn't a backbiter or a talebearer cause harm just as an adulterer? Doesn't a man or woman who cheats in their marriage kill the mind and heart just as a murderer kills the body? The reality is that it doesn't matter that I was branded a milkman's baby, God took that broken road from which I came and made my way straight.

But for those who are righteous, the way is not steep and rough. You are a God who does what is right, and you smooth out the path ahead of them. Lord, we show our trust in you by obeying your laws; our heart's desire is to glorify your name. In the night I search for you; in the morning I earnestly seek you. For only when you come to judge the earth will people learn what is right. Isaiah 26:7-9 (NLT)

Every valley shall be exalted, and every mountain and hill shall be made low; and the crooked shall be made straight, and the rough places plain. And the glory of the Lord shall be revealed, and all flesh shall see it together; for the mouth of the Lord hath spoken it. Isaiah 40:3-5 (KJ21)

Forgetting where I came from, never! I couldn't change it if I wanted to. Even if I could, what choice would I make, for nothing on this earth is perfect? Would I choose to live the life of a rich child whose parents can give them everything money can buy but can't buy off that demon that they let convince them to experiment with drugs? Or would I choose to be born of another race only to find out that if I'm not born on the right side of the track I'll only be labeled as trash? Maybe I'll be born of just the right parents and live in just the right house, in just the right neighborhood still needing to realize that I am in need of Jesus Christ as my Lord and Savior to live the only true Way! Honestly, nothing that's ever existed on this earth since the fall of Adam has been perfect, except when I stand completely in the presence of God! In His presence all wrongs fade and everything becomes possible. Loving my enemies becomes possible. Forgiving those that use me becomes possible. Looking into the mirror and admitting when I am wrong becomes possible. Emerging more and more Christ-like becomes reality.

    In 1998, when the Spirit of the Lord spoke to me to speak on the subject of "It Ain't Easy, but It's Necessary," I had no clue where that topic was taking me and how many lives it would affect. It has become an anthem in my life when the *whys* and *whens* surface, and when the Spirit has asked me to take one for the Team. It has been a phrase thrown back at me when complaining about tasks assigned me. It has been a springboard while pressing forward in life and an anchor when the fierceness of storms battled against me. Most of all, that slogan has been a comforter to me that God knows that living the Christian life in such an ungodly world ain't easy. That He understands that it's the ones you love most that hurt you the most and He knows how uncomfortable it is to be vulnerable. Throughout it all, I have come to realize that the big picture is far more vast than I can comprehend. That sometimes my suffering is for the sake of others not perishing, a small impersonation of Jesus. It's not easy, but as I praise God for my brother's eternal place in heaven, I realize that this is just the work that Jesus commissioned us to do when He said "Go!" I won't dare attempt to add to the Holy Word, but from the experiences I have lived may I include that as you go remember it won't be easy, but it is necessary that at some point you suffer for the sake of the gospel being a light to a dark world.

Acknowledgements

I would like to thank all the people who have given their time, prayers, and talents to help bring this book into reality.

Thank you to Pamela Simmons, who gave so much of her time in editing and advising me throughout this project. Your words were fuel to my hope, "Get the book published, someone needs this." You have heard the Spirit of God's voice through my writings for so many years and have carefully guided without eliminating the me in my writings. Many years ago you said you wanted to help with editing. I still remember the look on your face, I was honored. To include this project into your schedule with the many hats that you wear, is priceless. I am blessed to call you and your family friend.

Thanks to Harold Foster, Jr. for the creation of my book cover. I hope to work with you on many projects to come. God bless you

Thank you to Tina Rivera for giving your time and expertise in helping me get this project off the ground. Thank you for seeing the vision of God in my life. Thank you for hearing God when you opened the door for me to minister at the Thanksgiving Gala. It was the beginning of *"It Ain't Easy, But It's Necessary"*

Thanks to Contessa Taylor, my beautiful daughter in law, who took my dream and handled it with care as she proofread my writings. Working with you brought more depth to our relationship as I realized that you were not only my beloved daughter, but also a brilliant scholar of education. My heart swells with pride as the facet of who you are continue to unfold.

Thanks to Lula Davidson, my friend of many years. History between us has proven that God really does have a plan for everything all along. We stand, having weathered the storms of growth, working together on another project. You took my baby gently into your hands and with the eyes of God you helped correct imperfections that would have caused her to fall short of excellence. You are a rock and I'm grateful that God chose you to be a part of my life. You *heard* my story! Thank you!

Thanks you, to my Mom. Without your understanding this would have been an unpublished book. You allowed me to reveal our pains for the sake of helping others. Our latter days are better then our former days, thank you for seeing me. You are my jewel.

Thank you to my children, Reggie, Brian, and Jennifer for giving me your blessings in allowing my life to be transparent. Thank you for the times, during my transparency, you became transparent without shame.

To Miyoshi, my first born, thank you for excusing my blunders as I practiced being an adult, sometimes at your expense. I have never regretted your existence, I just wish I had given you another beginning. Forgive me for the things I missed, but please know, that as a child myself, I was learning as I went. But we made it, didn't we? It wasn't easy, but God was faithful to heal our hurts and take us both to higher grounds.

Thanks to my husband, Kevin, who allowed me the time needed to complete this task. Thank you for the sacrifices of our monies and for believing in the calling upon my life.

Thank you for understanding when I needed to give God my time. You helped make obeying God easy. Also, thank you for becoming the best "Pops" to my BratPack they could have ever had. Lastly, thank you for living through the details of my life before your existence. Thank you for putting them in their respective places and locking the vault that's labeled, "For God's Use Only."

All honor and glory goes to my Heavenly Father, my Savior and my Lord, my Teacher and my Guide who entrusted me with the calling of helping hurting people.

References

Copyrighted © 2015 by Mary J Pickens. All rights reserved. Any reproduction must be approved in writing. Send requests by email to: maryj@helpinghurtingpeople.com

All scriptures used are from the New Kings James Version unless otherwise indicated.

Scripture taken from the THE MESSAGE. Copyright 1993, 1994, 1995, 1996, 2000, 2001, 2002. Used by permission of NavPress Publishing Group

Scripture quotations marked NLT are taken from the Holy Bible, New Living Translation, copyright 1996, 2004. Used by permission of Tyndale House Publishers, Inc., Wheaton, Illinois 60189. All rights reserved

Scripture quotations taken from THE AMPLIFIED BIBLE, Copyright 1954, 1958, 1962, 1964, 1965, 1987 by The Lockman Foundation. All rights reserved. Used by permission. (www.Lockman.org)

Scripture quotations taken from the 21st Century King James Version, copyright 1994. Used by permission of Deuel Enterprises, Inc. Gary, SD 57237. All rights reserved.

Hinds' Feet on High Places by Hannah Hurnard, 1955

What's Love Got To Do With It -Tina Turner 1984

Sitting On The Dock Of The Bay - Otis Redding 1967

Blessed Assurance -Fanny J Crosby - 1873

Logo created for Mary J Pickens by Todd Dotty of Flair for Design (info@flairfordesign.com)

Book Cover designed by Harold D. Foster, Jr. (hdfosterjr@yahoo.com)

NOTES

To contact the author write:

Mary J Pickens Ministries

P. O. Box 8117

Shreveport, LA. 71148

Internet Address: www.helpinghurtingpeople.com

Email: maryj@helpinghurtingpeople.com

Please include your testimony or explanation of help received from this book when you write.

Your prayer requests are welcome

Made in the USA
Middletown, DE
15 February 2016